BASEBALL'S
Book of
FIRSTS

"Babe Ruth"   "Lou Gehrig"

BASEBALL'S
Book of
FIRSTS

by Lloyd Johnson

9 8 7 6 5 4 3 2 1
Digit on the right indicates the number of this printing.

Library of Congress Cataloging-in-Publication Number 98-72527

ISBN 0-7624-0477-9

Cover and interior book design by Beth A. Crowell
Photo Research by Sara Dunphy
Edited by Barbara Thrasher

This book may be ordered by mail from the publisher.
But try your bookstore first!

Published by Courage Books, an imprint of
Running Press Book Publishers
125 South Twenty-second Street
Philadelphia, Pennsylvania 19103-4399
Visit us on the web!
www.runningpress.com

PAGE 2: Babe Ruth and Lou Gehrig. The Yankees won three
straight pennants soon after Gehrig became a regular in 1925, hitting behind Ruth in the lineup.

THIS PAGE: The Rangers' Nolan Ryan thanks the fans, who have
just witnessed his historic 5,000th strikeout in 1989.

OPPOSITE:
Jackie Robinson's look of fierce concentration often intimidated
National League hurlers.

400

CONTENTS

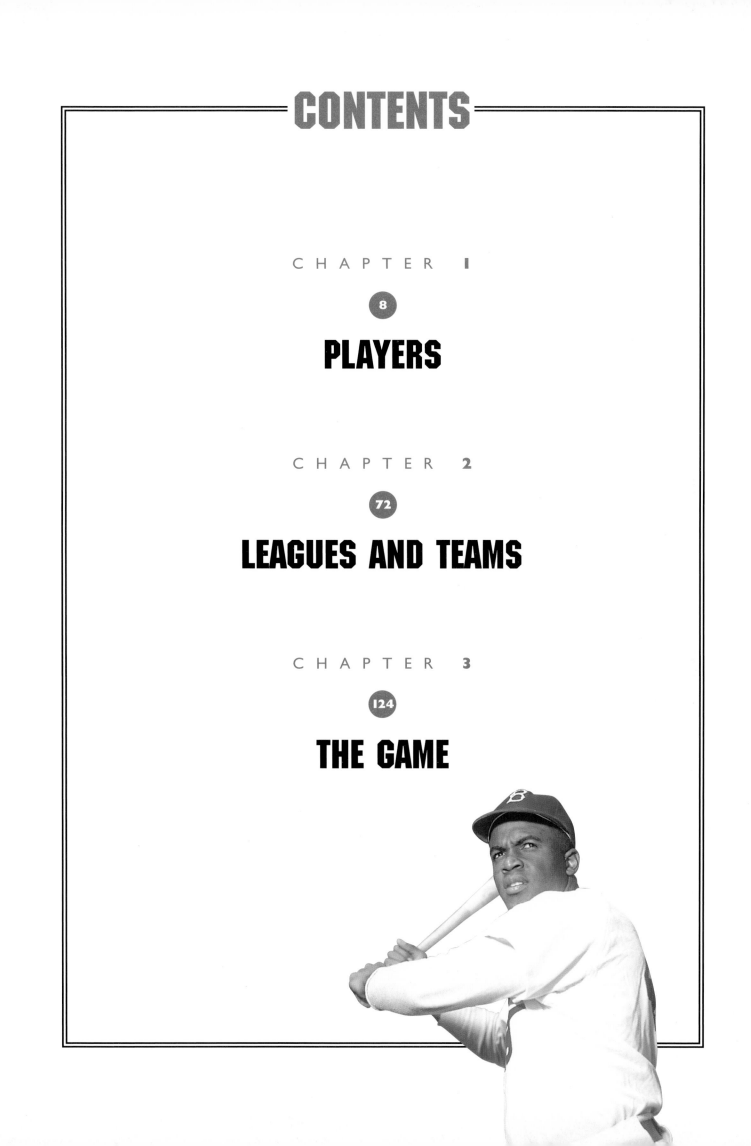

FOREWORD

As a graduate student I read and wrote comparative reports on dozens of books about the French Revolution. One characteristic jumped out at me. The historical interpretations of the Committee of Public Safety and the Reign of Terror varied greatly and were influenced by the time period in which they were written. One book, scribed in occupied France during the winter of the darkest days of World War II, presented a plausible scenario for the Reign of Terror and the Law of Suspects (guilt by accusation): Anything or any action can become "normal" and accepted if there are enough people who become blinded to the "big picture." This book is an attempt to create the "big picture" of baseball by unveiling the beginnings of many things that we take for granted in the sport, such as relay throws, cutoff plays, infield tarps, Ladies Days, seventh-inning stretches, and many more "firsts."

On the 100th anniversary of Babe Ruth's birthday Hofstra University held a party, and Ruthophiles came from the four corners of North America, plus Japan, to analyze and commemorate the career of baseball's most famous figure. I had the privilege to sit with an opening night panel of baseball scholars such as John Thorn, editor and founder of *Total Baseball*; Art Schott, the official "Baseball Historian" of Louisiana since 1956; Dan Okrent, main consultant for Ken Burns's film series on baseball, and one of the founders of Rotisserie Baseball; David Pietrusza, author/historian and president of the Society for American Baseball Research (SABR), and Robert Creamer, writer/historian and author of *The Babe*. When my turn came to speak, I said, "The Babe was fun. He made life fun. Something was always happening around the Babe. By demanding more money for himself he single-handedly raised every players' salary when he extended upper limits of the salary structure, a move that would increase the upper level possibilities. He made life better for all ballplayers, and he had fun doing it." After two hours of speeches Robert Creamer, the featured speaker, concurred — the Babe *was* fun.

In the spirit of Ruth and for all who want to see the "big picture," this book was written. I hope that the readers have as much fun as I did exploring the many firsts that have shaped baseball, sometimes in seemingly haphazard ways.

Organized by category, the 151 firsts in this volume include many accounts of contemporary achievements that parallel firsts. For example, the section about the first intentional walk explores the earliest recorded incident — in the 1886 World Championships — and the modern-day intentional walks record compiled by base threats Willie McCovey and Barry Bonds. These anecdotal narratives may benefit from an overview of early baseball history.

The first professional league was the National Association (1871–75). It dissolved and the National League (NL) was formed in 1876. Three rival leagues, International (IA), American (AA), and Union (UA) Associations, contested the NL for players and bragging rights. The AA was the only league that survived the birthing process and subsequent competition. It played the NL in a nineteenth-century World Series starting in 1882. The NL, AA and a minor league — Northwestern — signed an agreement that governed relations among the three. These rules and regulations and the enforcement of them became known as "Organized Ball" (O.B.). Those leagues which chose not to be part of the National Agreement were considered outlaw leagues, outside of O.B. The rules of O.B. governed player contracts, trades, transfers, drafts and releases; in another words and on a larger scale, it governed leagues' relationships to other leagues, teams' relations to other teams, and all player dealings. For self-protection, the players started a union in 1885.

Under the capable leadership of Hall of Fame pitcher/batter/manager John Montgomery Ward, the union flourished and led a players' strike that resulted in a new league — called the Players' League — being founded in 1890. The ensuing baseball war was one of attrition in which the players won all of the battles but the owners won the peace. The casualties were salaries, players' rights, the Players' League, and the American Association.

TOP: An overflow crowd at Boston's Huntington Avenue Grounds watches the final game of the 1903 World Series.
ABOVE: Giants manager John McGraw (left) relaxes with the Pirates' Honus Wagner in 1919 or 1920 after Wagner became a coach.
BELOW: The 1941 Chicago American Giants were led by Dave Malarcher, seated bottom row middle.

From 24 teams in three leagues in 1890, the majors shrunk to 12 teams in one league by 1892. The battle for roster positions in the 1890s fostered the ugliest time in baseball history as the players fought each other — and umpires, fans, cops and the other teams — for their existence. Out of the turmoil and savagery came the American League (AL).

Founded as the Western League in 1894 by Byron Ban Johnson, a young sportswriter originally from Cincinnati, the American League, as it came to be called in 1900, represented the principles of good, clean, honest and wholesome family entertainment. In order to secure talent, AL teams raided other leagues by offering higher salaries to experienced star players.

A baseball peace — established in 1903 — included the playing of an annual World Series. The period between 1903 and 1910 became known as the "Dead Ball" era, which ended when Shibe and Sons introduced the cork-centered baseball. The end of the "Dead Ball" era coincided with the beginning of the concrete-and-reinforced-steel ballpark building era. The old lovable giants — Crosley, Forbes, Shibe, Fenway, Comiskey, Ebbets, the Polo Grounds, Tiger Stadium and Griffith — became the nostalgic green cathedrals of baseball's "olden days." However, a part of baseball's lovable past did not include black players.

African-Americans could not play on the same fields as white major leaguers during the baseball season. In keeping with the law of the land — separate but equal — Andrew "Rube" Foster founded the Negro National League in 1920. After that white and black ballplayers frequently barnstormed together to make money. When World War II shortages affected the revenues of the major league club owners, they rented their parks to the Negro League teams. And the P. K. Wrigley-sponsored All-American Girls Professional Baseball League opened. When the war concluded baseball decided to integrate.

Integration of African-Americans into major league baseball might have been part of the drive to acquire players at cut-rate salaries — the idea had been the driving force behind baseball since 1871 when players first turned professional — but the new policy let Negro Leaguers on the playing field to show their abilities. The National League, particularly the Brooklyn Dodgers, gained the upper hand in signing Negro League players, causing the balance of power to swing toward the Senior Circuit. The AL had dominated All-Star and post-season play, on the strength of the New York Yankees, since the mid-1920s. The reason for Yankee dominance could be found in the front office.

New York (AL) utilized an idea from Branch Rickey called the farm system whereby major league clubs signed and trained young players by testing them at the minor league level for play in the majors. The Yankees had the most money and the best front office personnel, so they often dominated baseball from 1926 to 1965, when they were sold to CBS, a television network with limited experience at operating baseball clubs. The Yankees' subsequent decline was precipitated by the advent of the free-agent draft.

Less wealthy clubs, tired of being outbid for high school and amateur talent (the same reason that Branch Rickey started the farm system), proposed a club-by-club draft. Rick Monday of the Arizona University Wildcats was the first player chosen. He signed with the Oakland A's, and played 17 years. Once again the scouting system became responsible for finding and signing major league talent. The Oakland A's, led by owner Charles O. Finley, dominated baseball by making the best choices with regard to young talent. But when the older, more established stars saw money and attention turning toward unproven talent, they decided to do something about it.

The players, led by Jim Bunning and Robin Roberts, hired a labor leader and former negotiator for the steelworkers' union as executive director for its union in 1966. Marvin Miller and the players changed baseball history by demanding and getting their fair share of baseball revenues. Several strikes became necessary to influence club owners, who were not used to dealing with organized labor, into accepting a contract called "The Basic Agreement." The owners agreed to it, but never thought that they would actually have to adhere to it. The result was both chaotic and sensational. Never before had baseball enjoyed such prosperity, nor had it ever seen such high wages being paid to ballplayers.

Baseball has always been a game and a business. As you read this book of firsts, remember that baseball is not an easy game. In the whole history of the sport, only 160,000 men have played professional baseball. Of that number, only 16,000 made it to the majors. Of those who played major league baseball, only 146 have made it to the Baseball Hall of Fame, which was established in 1936 to honor the best in the game. Baseball is indeed a difficult game to play, and an even more difficult game in which to excel. The sport fosters the drive to succeed and the will to win, and that's why we call it "The National Pastime." And in this perpetual striving, there will always be new "firsts" to enhance the history of baseball.

Lloyd Johnson

ABOVE: Larry Doby poses on July 5, 1947, the day he became the first African-American in the American League. Earlier in the season, Doby played second base for the Newark Eagles of the Negro National League.

BELOW: World Series hero of 1997, the Marlins' Livan Hernandez delivers a pitch in the fifth inning of Game One.

WORLD'S SERIES 1933
GIANTS vs SENATORS
POLO GROUNDS, NEW YORK

PRICE 25 CENTS

PLAYERS

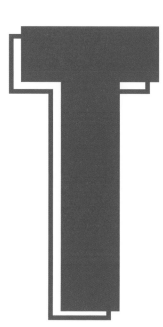

his section relates to achievement. Success in baseball is often measured by the accumulation of numbers or statistics. The statistics are compared from year to year, from player to player, and from era to era. We fans have the resources to do this mental exercise of measuring achievement because of the abundance of statistics and statistical books, and equally importantly, because of the three-way marriage of baseball, newspapers and statistics which occurred almost 150 years ago.

Since that time, the compendiums of baseball numbers have advanced from the Beadle *Dime Player* (1860) to the *Baseball Cyclopedia* (1922), edited by Ernest J. Lanigan, to Thompson and Turkin's *Encyclopedia of Baseball* (1948), to *The Baseball Encyclopedia* (1969), published by Macmillan (called affectionately "Big Mac"), to the comprehensive stat book, *Total Baseball*. The numbers in this section and throughout the book are consistent with those in *Total Baseball*, but some of the figures are subject to change.

There are several on-going projects by members of the Society for American Baseball Research always adding to the total body of baseball knowledge. An especially significant one is the retroactive gathering of data for RBI, hits by pitcher, and stolen bases during the nineteenth and early twentieth centuries. For example, Paul Hines, Tip O'Neill, Hugh Duffy, Heine Zimmerman, Ty Cobb and Nap Lajoie became Triple Crown winners after the fact, due to the collection of RBI data.

In pre-professional nineteenth-century baseball, statistics were reported differently than they are today. The statistics of note were runs per game, hits per game and outs per game; eventually the focus evolved to the batting average stat. For example, Dickey Pearce averaged 3.5 runs/game and 1.8 outs/game in 1859. Jim Creighton was 2.4 and 2.8 in 1860. Team names and nicknames were also different. The baseball clubs were truly membership organizations. For example, the Athletic Base Ball Club of Philadelphia had several teams. The First Nine represented the club in outside matches. Most clubs had exercises in which members of the group played baseball among themselves. The structure of team nicknames can be illustrated with the White Stocking Base Ball Club of Chicago, which became the Chicago White Stockings. Later, club officials or newspapermen changed their name to Colts, Orphans, and finally Cubs.

Please enjoy reading of the game's greatest innovators and achievers among the players, managers, umpires and officials.

LEFT: The 1933 World Series program featured a composite drawing instead of a photograph.
BELOW: Lou Gehrig scores on his 1937 All-Star Game home run off Dizzy Dean. On the next pitch, Dean was hit on the big toe by a line drive off the bat of Earl Averill. Dean's career was shortened because of the injury.

Batters

The First Superstar Batter
He Never Made an Out

1862

Jim Creighton's phenomenal success made him the most imitated player of his era. Boys mimicked the way he walked, the way he batted, and the way he threw the ball with a little wrist spin. The 1860s wrist spin controversy equaled the "split-finger" fastball controversy of the 1980s.

Jim Creighton became baseball's first superstar when the sport was in its infancy. He pitched an amazingly swift low fastball underhanded. The leading rule makers of the day met to view and discuss his pitching style. It was unanimous among the leaders of the national game that Creighton's style of pitching fell within the rules. His club took him on a road trip to upstate New York. Afterwards, he became the imitated player of his day. Boys formed Creighton Base Ball Clubs. At the height of popularity, he compiled the greatest season ever and died, all at the age of 21.

In 1862, Creighton did not make an out for the entire season. He averaged 4.2 runs per game. He pitched and batted leadoff for the Excelsior Base Ball Club. Creighton never lived to collect on his wondrous year. He died as the result of hitting a game-winning home run.

On October 18, 1862, Creighton swung hard at a pitch and heard something pop so loudly that the on-deck batter, John "Death to Flying Things" Chapman, heard it also. Creighton ran out his hit, thinking that his belt had snapped. He crossed home plate and collapsed. Apparently an internal organ had ruptured. He lay in agony for two days and then expired at the age of 21 years, seven months, and two days.

Jim Creighton first showed fans and businessmen the marketing power of star quality players. He proved that a single player had enough drawing power to carry a franchise, a truth that would still reverberate at the end of the next century with drawing cards like Ken Griffey, Jr. and Mark McGwire.

The First Batter to Gain 3,000 Hits
Hit King

1894

BELOW RIGHT: Cap Anson's autobiography, *A Ball Players' Career*, revealed baseball history through the eyes of the nineteenth century's best player.

BELOW LEFT: *Born to Hit* was the name of George Brett's biography. The curly-haired bachelor turned on Kansas City fans with his run at .400 in 1980.

Who was the first 3,000 hit man? He was the best player of the nineteenth century, and he was named for two Roman emperors. Adrian Constantine "Cap" Anson's hit total has fluctuated with each publication of new data. During the "Big Mac" years (*The Baseball Encyclopedia* by Macmillan) Anson was listed with 3,041 hits, with 430 more from his National Association (NA) days. The current edition of *Total Baseball* places Anson at 2,995, with 423 more in the NA. Nonetheless, Anson's 3,418 hits in 27 years provided the benchmark by which future hitters would be judged.

History had to give credit to Honus Wagner and Larry Lajoie, because contemporary writers gave them little ink when they topped the 3,000 hit mark in 1914. Likewise, Ty Cobb received no fanfare when he passed the vaunted mark in 1921. However, three years later, when the Georgian surpassed Honus Wagner on the hit parade, he finally received front page stories. Toiling in obscurity was not just the problem of baseball's early days.

When George Brett reached 3,000 in 1992 with the aid of a magical four-for-four night on the West Coast, barely 300 Kansas City fans were still awake for the West Coast radio broadcast. Likewise, when Paul Molitor socked his benchmark hit in 1996 — a rippling triple to the right-center field wall — it was before a sparse crowd of less than 8,000. As Brett and Molitor proved, hits wait for no media. The media and fans must be ready for the milestone.

The First Batter
to Hit 500 Home Runs
The Sultan of Swat

1929

The mighty Sultan of Swat passed Roger Conner for the major league career home run leadership in 1921, his third year of full-time play. The incomparable Babe Ruth remained the career leader until Hank Aaron broke his 714 mark in 1974. As the first to reach 300, 400, 500, 600 and 700 home runs, Ruth withstood assaults from all comers. Jimmie Foxx, Mel Ott, Ted Williams, plus many of Aaron's contemporaries such as teammate Eddie Mathews, Ernie Banks, Frank Robinson, Willie Mays (660 in 22 years despite playing several years in the Negro Leagues as a teenager), Mickey Mantle, Willie McCovey, Reggie Jackson and Mike Schmidt, joined the 500 home run club. Only Aaron and Ruth share the 700 club.

Baseball in the 1970s needed Hank Aaron. Mickey Mantle had retired and Willie Mays was in the shadows of a brilliant career. Stan Musial and Ted Williams had been gone for 10 years. Aaron was the man. The shy, southern slugger had been one of baseball's most productive players during the 1950s and 1960s, but never had received the accolades from fans or press. His teammates were stars; he was just the best player. As the Braves' slugger passed the 600 and 700 levels, baseball realized that Babe Ruth's lifetime home run record would fall. They were caught unaware. Aaron had, without fanfare and hoopla, walloped 40 or more four-baggers eight times, and 30 or more 15 times. Passing 700, he had hit 24 or more home runs for 19 consecutive years. His final clout of the 1973 season was home run number 713, one behind the Babe.

All winter Aaron had to endure the most racist hate mail in the history of baseball. As soon as the season started he wasted no time in connecting off Jack Billingham to tie the Bambino. Four days later, in the Braves' home opener, Aaron blasted an Al Downing pitch into the left-center field bullpen area. There was a new home run king, and his name was Henry Louis Aaron.

The First Batter to Get 100 Hits From Each Side of the Plate
The Switch-Hit Parade

1979

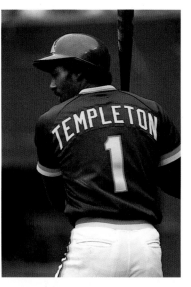

Success from lefty-righty batter versus pitcher platooning was well-known and utilized by Giants manager John McGraw. Another platoon manager, Casey Stengel, had batted .368 and .323 as platooned outfielder for the Giants. The future Ol' Perfessor never forgot his early lesson at the knee of John McGraw. When the Yankees under Stengel began to have success with Billy Johnson and Bobby Brown at third base and Gene Woodling and Hank Bauer in the outfield, youth coaches wondered if switch hitters would have a better chance to stay in the bigs.

Switch-hitting Garry Templeton threatened to make Cardinal fans forget about their first switch hitter, Frank Frisch. The 5'11" shortstop filled every scouts' dream. He was rangy with a little power. By 1979, Templeton put all of his skills together as he spanked 100 hits from each side of the plate en route to a season average of .314, with league-leading marks of 211 hits and 19 triples. He had to bat exclusively right-handed for the last nine games of the season to make his record. Willie Wilson, the speed merchant of the Kansas City Royals, watched Templeton and realized that he could accomplish the same feat.

The next year, Willie Wilson used 705 official at-bats (second highest total of all time) to achieve 100 hits from each side of the plate. As with Garry Templeton, Wilson was forced to bat right-handed against righty pitchers to achieve the record.

Nonetheless, the fleet leadoff batter amassed 230 hits, good for 133 runs and 79 stolen bases. In some ways, the Templeton and Wilson achievement proved that records can be broken if a player fixes on a record suited to his skills, and pursues it with dogged determination.

The First Batter to Reach 175 RBI

The Rain of RBI

1927

TOP: Lou Gehrig cracked 175 RBI in 1927. The secret to his power is shown in his open stance, with his bat back.

INSET: Hank Greenberg failed to impress Yankee and Giant scouts as a youngster from the Bronx. The Tigers' RBI king proved that power sluggers take longer to develop than singles hitters.

The big talk in 1927 was not Babe Ruth's home run record — he had already hit 54 and 59 in consecutive seasons — but Lou Gehrig's assault on the 200 RBI barrier. Larrapin' Lou kept home run pace with the Bambino until September, when the former Red Sox pitcher-turned-slugger belted 17 more, taking runners off base for the next hitter Gehrig. "Biscuit pants," as he was affectionately known, finished with 175 RBI in 155 games

Gehrig later clubbed American League pitching for 184 ribbies in 1931, a major league mark that Hank Greenberg of the Tigers would challenge with 183 in 1937. Meanwhile in the National League in 1930, the Cubs' Hack Wilson — so named because of his physical resemblance to Hackenschmidt, the most notable wrestler of the era — took advantage of a near season-long injury to teammate Rogers Hornsby, the National League's greatest batsman who batted third in front of him. Instead of the extra-base hits raining off Hornsby's bat, Wilson stroked 183 singles and doubles, plus walked 100 times. Hack Wilson drove in more runs — 190 — than any player in major league baseball history.

The First Batter to Hit .400
Beating the Odds, and the Ball

1871

TOP LEFT: Rogers
Hornsby was the premier
NL power hitter during
the 1920s, and set the
modern NL batting record
with .424 in 1924.
TOP RIGHT: Hugh Duffy
set the major league
record with .440 in 1894.
NEXT PAGE: Long Levi
Meyerle, pictured here on
a Mort Rogers scorecard,
proved that one had
to be more than a hitter
to stick in the big leagues,
even in the 1870s.

Jim Creighton never made an out in 1862. George Wright walloped .587 against amateur and professional pitching in 1869. But the first batter to hit .400 against professional pitching would be Levi Meyerle of the Philadelphia Athletics. He was a good hitter and notorious fielder. After his 1871 season when he hit .492 to lead the league, he lost his third base position to a better fielder. Old Levi, or Long Lou as he was known, had fielded .648. He didn't cut the mustard by nineteenth-century fielding standards!

The modern National League batting record was established by Rogers Hornsby, who walloped .424 in 1924. He challenged Hugh Duffy, whose .440 for Boston in 1894 still stands as the overall National League and major league record. Duffy had the advantage of facing pitchers while they were trying to adjust to the 60'6" pitching distance, from the previous distance of 50 feet. When Duffy had his big season, the entire league hit .309. The Phillies started a .400 hitting outfield. Substitute Tuck Turner had the highest average at .416, Big Ed Delehanty and Big Sam Thompson were close behind at .407. Both drove home Sliding Billy Hamilton 192 times. Hamilton batted only .404, but pushed his on-base percentage to a league-leading .523. Duffy won the Triple Crown that year as slugging Boston edged out slugging Philadelphia for third place in a pennant race won by the 'Old Orioles' from Baltimore.

The last batter to break the .400 barrier was the Red Sox' Ted Williams, who batted .406 in 1941.

MORT. ROGERS'
BASE BALL
PHOTOGRAPHIC CARD

LEVI S. MEYERLE,
Base, Athletic Club, Philadelphia

PHOTOGRAPHED BY
J.W. BLACK, 173 WASHᴺ ST, BOSTON

PRICE 10 CTS.

PATENT APPLIED FOR

The First 30-30 and 40-40 Men
Speed and Power

1922
1988

BELOW: Willie Mays, Bobby Bonds, Andre Dawson, and Barry Bonds could hold a seminar on power and speed. The three retired stars stole 1,113 bases and whacked 1,430 home runs among them, while Barry passed the 400 mark for both categories in 1998.

RIGHT: Jose Canseco reached a new major league mark in 1988 — 42 homers and 40 stolen bases.

On September 23, 1988, Jose Canseco — outfielder and local heart throb of the Oakland Athletics — stole two bases (numbers 39 and 40) and smashed his 41st home run of the year, becoming the charter member of the 40-40 club. That's 40 home runs and 40 stolen bases. Later Barry Bonds turned the trick in 1996 after making the 30-30 mark three times.. He was following in his father's footsteps, as Bobby Bonds had hit the vaunted marks five times in 14 years.

The very first 30-30 guy was Ken Williams, the outfield star of the 1922 St. Louis Browns, a team that lost the American League pennant by a mere game. Williams whacked 39 homers

and stole 37 bases as George Sisler, Jack Tobin, Baby Doll Jacobsen and Urban Shocker led the Browns to their most wins ever. Williams never again approached the magical 30-30 marks. It would be the 1950s before another would reach those numbers, and his name would be Willie Mays. He achieved 30-30 two years in a row, in 1956 and 1957.

The First Batter to Win the Triple Crown
The Threes are Wild

1878

TOP LEFT: Cleveland manager Lou Boudreau devised a defensive shift that he hoped would counter the hitting ability of Boston's great slugger, Ted Williams.
TOP RIGHT: Ted Williams won the Triple Crown in 1942 and 1947.
BELOW RIGHT: Red Sox left fielder Carl Yazstremski was the heart and soul (and the big bat) of Boston's pennant-winning team in 1967, the year he won the Triple Crown.

Paul Hines of Providence had one great year: 1878. He turned an unassisted triple play as an outfielder, and led all National League batters with a .358 batting average, four home runs and 50 RBI. His slugging average was tops at .486. He was also partially deaf and had to wait 90 years for his batting title. Abner Dalrymple went to his grave in 1939 believing that he was the 1878 batting champ. However, the statistics from two tie games had not been counted. When the ties were included, per scoring rules of the day, Hines won the 1878 batting title. *Total Baseball* recognized Hines as the highest average and Dalrymple as the batting champ, but with a lower average.

The situation was much clearer in the 1920s when Rogers Hornsby dominated the National League scene with two Triple Crowns, and in the 1940s when Ted Williams did the same to American League pitching. Hornsby's two Triple Crown seasons occurred in 1922 (.401, 42, 152) and 1925 (.403, 39, 143). The Rajah's two crowns were mirrored by the pair won by Ted Williams, the Splendid Splinter of the Boston Red Sox. Terrible Ted overwhelmed American League pitchers with .356, 36, 137 in 1942 and .343, 32, 114 after the war in 1947.

Williams was great, but for sheer drama, another player stands out in Red Sox history, during the Impossible Dream year of 1967. The haunting "Impossible Dream" song from the popular musical *Man of La Mancha* was taken by Red Sox fans as their theme song when the Red Sox battled the Twins, White Sox and Detroit for the 1967 American League title. Carl Yazstremski went 4-for-4 in the season finale as Boston edged Minnesota 5-3 for first place. Yaz had 10 hits in his last 13 at-bats to capture the Triple Crown (.336, 44, 121) and lead the Red Sox to their first World Series since 1946.

Three Top Hitting Streaks
Eyes on the Prize

1897
1941
1978

BELOW LEFT: Wee Willie Keeler turned in a 44-game hitting streak in 1897. The second toughest batter in baseball history to fan, Keeler also hit .424 in 1897.

BELOW RIGHT: Joe DiMaggio's style remained unruffled even in the pressure of a batting streak, demonstrated by this home run swing on June 17, 1941 (game 37).

The National League record 44-game hitting streak (Willie Keeler with Baltimore in 1897) was an unknown record until 1922, when George Sisler compiled a 41-game hitting streak. Keeler had batted .432 with 243 hits in 128 games for the National League benchmark, tied by Pete Rose in 1978. Keeler's streak went down on June 18, when Baltimore's 3,856 fans saw Pittsburgh lefty Frank Killen shut Keeler out 0 for 4. Oddly, Keeler batted only .421 during his streak, which was lower than his seasonal average.

The Keeler mark was shattered by Joe DiMaggio in the summer of 1941. The Yankee Clipper hit safely in 56 consecutive games, surpassing all major league records. Several times, DiMaggio had close calls. Once he lifted a routine fly to right which fell at Pete Fox's feet. Another time, grounders to shortstop Luke Appling were booted and the Yankee Clipper beat the throws to first. The end of the streak came unexpectedly as DiMaggio smashed two vicious shots at third baseman Ken Keltner, who made sensational plays to nip the Clipper at first. Then shortstop Lou Boudreau took a bad hop and turned it into a double play. DiMaggio's run was over. He had hit .408 with 15 homers and 55 RBI during the streak.

Another streaker, Pete Rose, opened the 1978 season by lining a single — hit number 3,000 — to left field off Montreal's Steve Rogers. On June 14, the Reds' 16-year veteran began the hitting streak that would put him into the National League record books. Six times Rose extended the streak in his final at-bat. Four times his only hit was a bunt. Twice a bunt rescued him in his final at-bat. On July 24 at New York, Rose lined a seventh-inning single to left to equal the modern National League record of 37 games established in 1945 by Boston's Tommy Holmes. One night later Rose celebrated with Holmes after he singled to left off Craig Swan to set the new mark. Rose tied Keeler's mark of 44 straight games with a ground single to right field in the sixth inning off Phil Niekro in Atlanta on July 31. The next night, Braves pitching duo Larry McWilliams and Gene Garber held Rose without a hit. His last chance was in the ninth inning. With a 2-2 count, Pete tipped Garber's next delivery into the catcher's mitt for the third strike and final out. Rose had hit .385 during his record run.

The First Designated Hitter

Bloomin' Blomberg

1973

A's manager Connie Mack
(right) sits on the bench
with three of his pitchers,
Jack Coombs, Eddie Plank
and Boardwalk Brown.
Frustration with his pitchers' hitting led Mack to
propose the designated
hitter in 1905 — an idea
ahead of its time.

The Designated Hitter (DH) was first proposed by Connie Mack, skipper for the 1905 Philadelphia Athletics. The rumors were that he grew weary of watching Eddie Plank and Charles Bender flail away at pitches and call it batting. Mack's innovative proposal received little support and was even lambasted by the press as "wrong theoretically." But, the idea did not die.

National League President John Heydler revived the idea, but chose the wrong year. He called for it in 1930, the year that the last place Phillies batted .324 as a team. The National League did not even vote on it, but did vote to alter the ball by lowering the height of the stitches, which resulted in pitchers not be able to curve the ball. The American League was left to carry out the proposal of one of its founders 68 years earlier.

On Opening Day, April 6, 1973, Ron Blomberg, the sixth batter in the New York Yankees' lineup, walked with the bases loaded off Luis Tiant in the first inning. He did not have a field position. He was the first DH to bat, originally called Designated Pinch Hitter. The opposing Red Sox DH was Orlando Cepeda. Other DHs in the other day game were Terry Crowley, who batted eighth for the Orioles, and Ollie "Downtown" Brown for the Brewers. Brown batted in the six hole. The first DH Blomberg played in 100 games that season, 55 as DH. He hit a career-high .329.

The First to Hit 60 Homers, the First Teammates to Hit 50 Each, and the First to Blast 70

Home Run Derby

1920
1961
1998

BELOW: Yankees manager Miller Huggins shakes hands with Babe Ruth. The Yankee slugger set his long-standing 60 homer mark in 1927.
BOTTOM RIGHT: Roger Maris and Mickey Mantle lived together during the record-breaking 1961 season, blasting 115 home runs between them.

When the Yankees' Babe Ruth swatted 54 homers in 1920, he personally outpaced every team total in the American League. When he smacked 59 the next season, he again surpassed five of the seven league teams. For those two years, Ruth slugged 13 percent of all home runs hit in the Junior Circuit. It wasn't just that he hit home runs, it was the way he hit home runs that brought fans out. Then in 1927 he belted 60 roundtrippers, a record thought untouchable.

Ruth hit towering fly balls; some flew over the fence while others fell safely past outfielders who gamely tried to judge the uncatchable skyscrapers. Contrast the Bambino's impact with that of the first teammates to hit 50 a piece.

Roger Maris and Mickey Mantle battled all summer in 1961 against Babe Ruth's ghost. Previous attempts at the 60 home run mark wilted under the pressure of Ruth's 17 September home runs. Mantle was the fan favorite, and Maris incurred the wrath of the baseball faithful by banging 51 home runs by September 1. Then the Commissioner Ford Frick, who had ghostwritten articles for Ruth, made a historic ruling. Frick announced that if Maris broke Ruth's record he would have to do it in the same number of games as Ruth, or his record would have an asterisk beside his name. The ruling gave Maris the appeal of the underdog, but fans still wanted Mantle to break Ruth's record. Then Mantle suffered an injury, forcing him from the lineup. Maris kept going with Mantle cheering him on.

When the dust of 1961 had cleared the M & M boys had swatted 115 roundtrippers (Maris 61 and Mantle 54) as the Yankees won 109 games plus the World Series from Cincinnati. Roger Maris claimed the MVP Award as he broke Babe Ruth's cherished 60 home run record amidst the glare of TV cameras and to the consternation of much of the baseball establishment.

A new chapter was written in 1998, when a frenzied finish to an exciting home run race came as Mark McGwire belted his awe-inspiring 70th homer on the last day of the season. The Cubs' Sammy Sosa kept pace, ending with 66 in a season that featured a record four 50-homer hitters.

RIGHT: Mark McGwire and Sammy Sosa share a moment at first base during the Cardinals-Cubs game at Busch Stadium in which McGwire hit his record-breaking 62nd home run of the season. The two power-hitters challenged each other all during 1998, Sosa ending with 66 homers to McGwire's 70.

BOTTOM: Elation and hugs follow McGwire's historic 62nd homer at Busch Stadium on September 9, 1998.

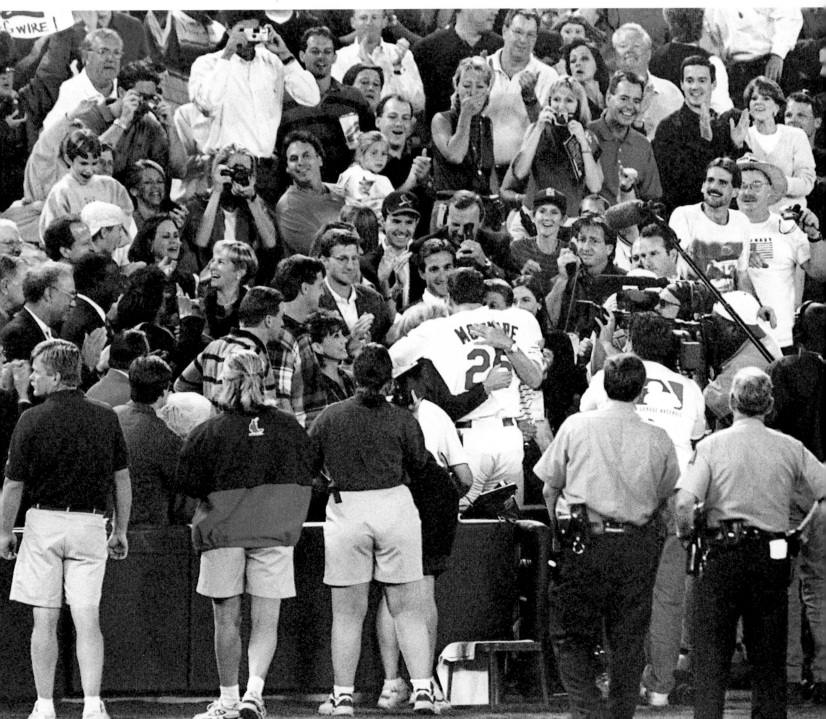

Fielders

The First Shortstop to Move Behind the Pitcher

Where is that Shortstop?

1849

The 1865 champion Brooklyn Atlantics featured Dickey Pearce (third from left), the innovative fielder credited with being the first shortstop to move behind the pitcher.

The advent of the short fielder, or shortstop, was a crucial break in the early game of rounders, nudging it toward baseball. The position was created in 1849 or 1850 by Dr. Daniel Adams of the Knickerbockers. He related, "I used to play shortstop and I believe I was the first one to occupy that place, as it had formerly been left uncovered." When Adams first went out to short, it was not to bolster the infield but to assist in relay throws from the outfield. The early Knickerbocker ball was so light that it could not be thrown far, thus the need for a short fielder to return the ball to the pitcher's points.

One of the earliest and most skillful shortstops was Dickey Pearce, an innovative and long lived player with the Brooklyn Atlantics. At 5' 3½" and 165 pounds, Pearce was short and pudgy. As early as 1855 his chunky little form was flying about the diamond, covering more ground than anyone thought possible. His innovative play made the Atlantics the premier team in New York City. Pearce represented Brooklyn in the Fashion Race Course All-Star games of 1858. He even caught Jim Creighton in 1861. For more than 20 years, except three or four years of George Wright's best seasons, Pearce was the premier player at his position.

The *Spalding Guide* of 1878 stated the importance of the position as, "With one or more men on bases, it is almost impossible for a ball to be hit without some intelligent and prompt movement being required of the shortstop in the way of backing up, and we would urge all players who would succeed in this position to make a study of this feature."

The First Catcher to Move Up for Every Pitch
A Thinking Man's Game

1887

Refinements in pitching rules and improvements with catcher's gear during the 1880s changed the game. When overhand pitching became legal, the curveball emerged as a weapon. The overhand curve broke down, causing the batter to consistently swing over the pitch. The catcher had to move closer to snag it before the throw hit the dirt. At the same time, improvements in protection — mask, chest protector and glove — enabled the receiver to crouch behind the batter without being injured.

When Connie Mack started his baseball career as a rail-thin catcher during the 1880s, he stood 10 to 20 feet behind the batter. His pitcher fired the ball high and inside, trying to get the batter to tip the ball where the angular Mack could leap and snare it. Many agile players, such as King Kelly, Dickey Pearce and Cap Anson, spent several seasons behind the plate. Deacon White of the Cleveland Forest City club was one of the first receivers to move up behind the batter. But midway into the 1887 season, Charles "Chief" Zimmer decided to move behind the batter for every pitch. The up close position enabled him to encourage the pitchers who needed it, because during that season batters received an extra strike and bases on balls were counted as hits.

Zimmer was not an ordinary receiver. He was a college man, matriculated at Carlisle College. He was also an officer of the Brotherhood, he was involved with John M. Ward, Tim Keefe and Fred Pfeffer, the intelligentsia of nineteenth-century baseball. As the catcher for wild and crazy Cleveland Spiders, he played a major role in the development of Cy Young from a country bumpkin to a first class hurler. Zimmer went to Pittsburgh where he shared catching duties with Jack "Peach Pie" O'Connor, anchoring a three-time pennant winner. Zimmer's play behind the plate enabled catchers to effectively control a baseball game and established him as one of the most innovative catchers in baseball history.

The First Third Baseman
to Charge Bunts
The Hot Corner, Revisited

1890s

Jimmy Collins still holds the single-season NL record for total chances (601 in 1899) and putouts (252 in 1900) by a third baseman. Considered one of baseball's brainiest players, he led the neophyte Boston Red Sox to two AL pennants and a victory in the first modern World Series.

Prior to Jimmy Collins — third base star with Boston in both the National and American Leagues at the turn of the century — a batter who laid a bunt down toward third easily beat the throw to first. The third baseman had no defense against the bunt, until Collins changed the way the position was fielded. He would charge forward with an all-out dash to scoop and whip the ball to first with an underhanded snap throw. With his technique, Collins consistently led third basemen in assists and total chances per game, and also in double plays. Other third sackers played back.

Third base was coined the "hot corner" in the 1880s by newspaperman Ren Mulford, who watched Cincinnati third sacker Hick Carpenter attempt to field shot after shot as the visitors peppered him all day long. Carpenter played more than 1,000 games at the "hot corner" despite being left-handed.

The hot corner grew to a glamour position. Ken Keltner of the Cleveland Indians made two sterling stops and throws to end Joe DiMaggio's 56-game hitting streak in 1941. Baltimore's Brooks Robinson used the 1970 World Series to showcase his fielding talents. Robinson stymied the favored Cincinnati Reds with an unbelievable backhand stab and throw out of Lee May in the Series opener that prevented a Reds rally. The Orioles won the game. Game Three featured fielding gems by Robinson in the first, second and sixth innings. His great plays were seen by a nation-wide television audience that numbered 50 million.

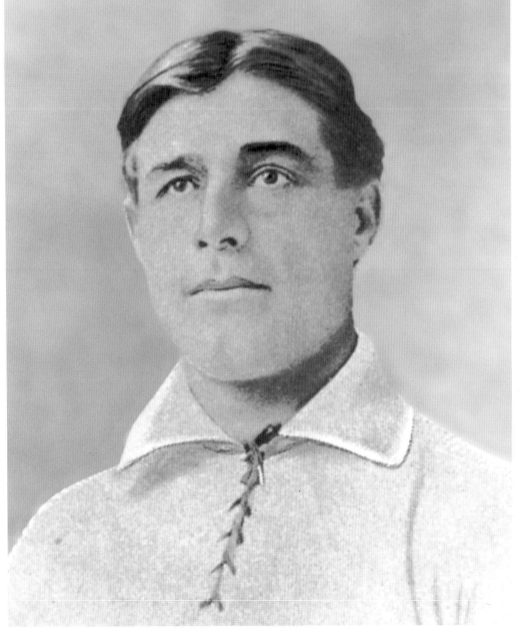

BELOW: The Mets' first baseman Keith Hernandez was known for his fielding, but he also hit .344 in 1979. **RIGHT:** Charles Comiskey began his professional career in 1879 with promoter Ted Sullivan in the Northwest League. The two men started the St. Louis AA franchise in 1882, where Comiskey held down first base and began to play off the bag.

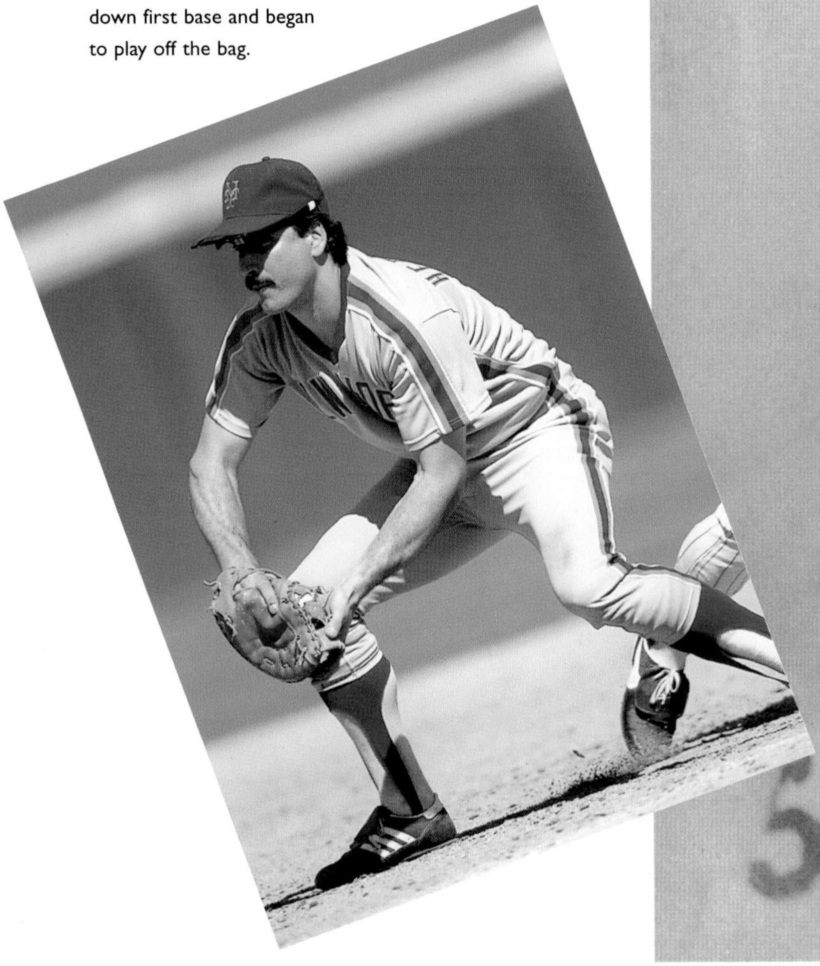

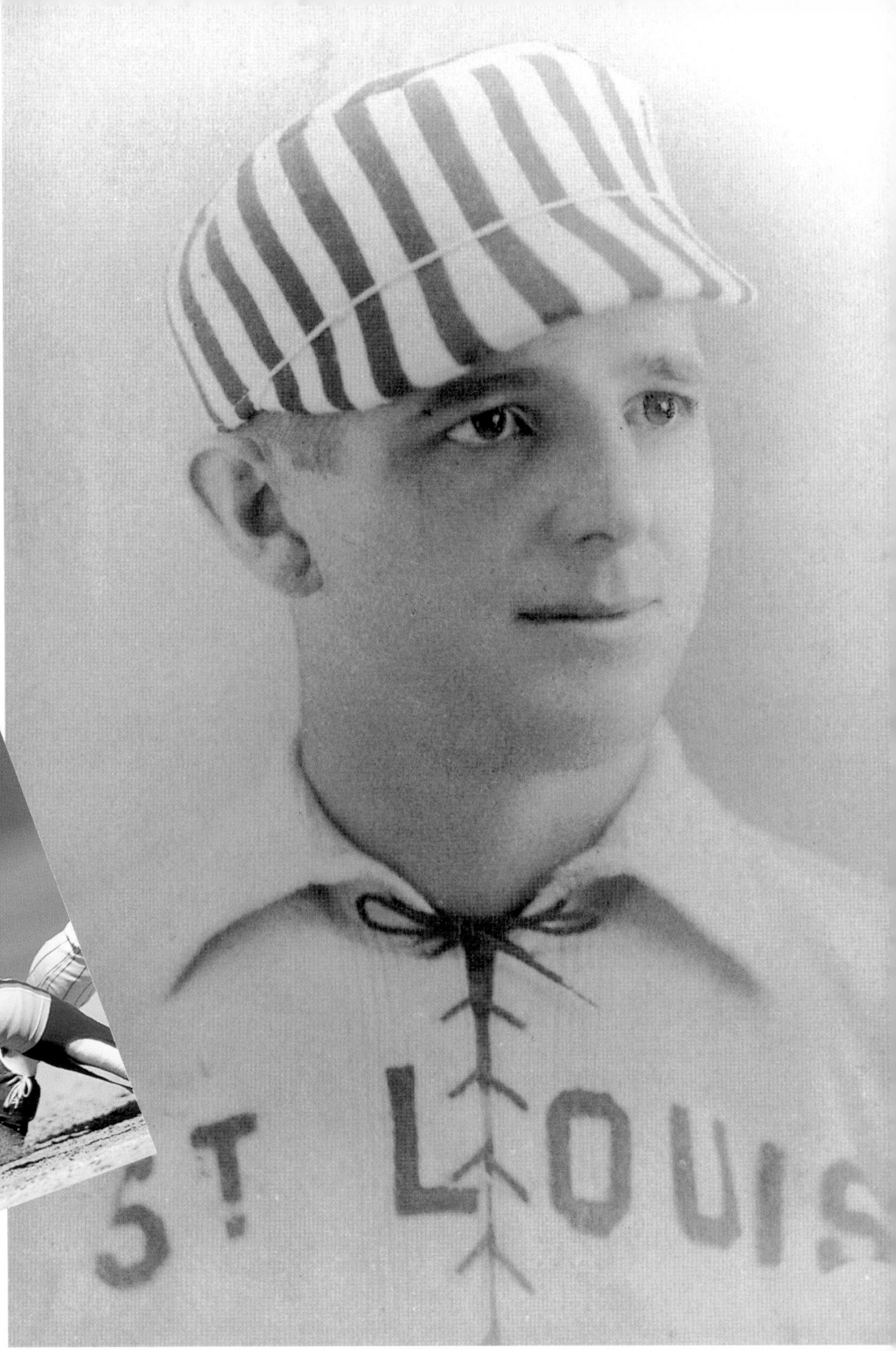

The First First Baseman to Leave the Bag

Covering More Ground

1880s

Joe Start, the reliable first baseman for the New York Mutuals and the Providence Grays, receives credit for standing one step off the first base bag. He was the first to move off the bag, but not very far. With fielding in the nineteenth century more important than slugging, St. Louis first sacker Charles Comiskey was the first to play the nearly modern position. He grew tired of leaving a gaping hole behind first and second bases when the second sacker went to cover on a steal, so he moved as far off the base as he could and still get back in time to catch the throw.

First base had its share of innovative performers, from Comiskey in the 1880s who moved off the bag to cover more ground, to Hal Chase (1910s) and Keith Hernandez (1980s), both known for charging ground balls and bunts while making plays to third base. Both were known to field bunted balls on the third base side of the diamond, yet they were able to stop a drive from the batter who would fake a bunt and line the ball directly at the fielder.

The First Gold Glove Winners
Holy Mitts!

1957

Thirty-three years after the awards first began, Ken Griffey Jr. and Harold Reynolds celebrate their Gold Glove Awards in 1990. It was Junior's first and Reynolds' last Gold Glove. Reynolds went on to become a well-known ESPN Sports Center host.

n 1950 members of the Baseball Writers Association of America (BBWAA) voted for the greatest all-time baseball team. The stars were primarily from the 1910-40 era. A Ty Cobb interview expressed the feeling of the old-timers that current players were not as good as the ones from his era. "Only one player could have played with us," boasted Cobb, "and that player is Phil Rizzuto." The Scooter, who could field and bunt with the best shortstops, was hardly the number one performer of his day. Cobb's comment started sportswriters to thinking about who and what were important in baseball. They came to the conclusion that pitching and fielding were being overlooked, and that all of the awards honored batting.

In 1955 the Cy Young Award was established to honor the best pitcher that year. Then in 1957 the Gold Glove Award was inaugurated to honor the best fielder at each position. After that year the awards went to the best in each league, whereas in the beginning the award honored the best nine players regardless of league affiliation. The first honorees (best fielders at their positions) were Bobby Shantz, pitcher; Sherman Lollar, catcher; Gil Hodges, first base; Nellie Fox, second base; Frank Malzone, third base; Roy McMillan, shortstop; plus Willie Mays, Minnie Minoso and Al Kaline in the outfield.

Pitchers

FIRST THE NINE.

The First "Ace" Pitcher
Our Asa

1896

Asa Brainerd, standing on the left, is pictured with The First Nine — the 1868 Cincinnati Base Ball Club. The Reds' ace hurled 65 straight wins.

The highest card in the playing deck was the "ace." The fighter pilot who shot down at least five enemy aircraft became an "ace." The number one pitcher on a team was known as the "ace" of the staff. All of these definitions lead backward to Asa Brainerd, the pitcher of the Cincinnati Red Stockings from 1869 to 1870. As the best pitcher for the best team in baseball and winner of at least 65 straight contests Asa became famous. According to legend, teams during the 1870s referred to their box men as "our Asa" and to rival hurlers as "their Asa." Quickly Asa changed into "Ace."

The nickname has fallen into disuse. Perhaps the moniker "Ace" placed too much pressure on its bearer. The last players to be called such were Willis "Ace" Hudlin and Clarence "Ace" Parker, though Parker's nickname came more from his football prowess than from his pitching.

The First Pitcher to Use a Curveball

The Pitcher has a Crooked Eye

1860s

Legends were made with curveballs. The rookie wrote home, "Mom, I'll be back soon. They started throwing curveballs." Zane Grey wrote three baseball books. One, *The Shortstop*, was a story about a young man who played baseball, but was chased out of towns because he was ugly and had a deformed eye. The man, Chase Alloway, pitched for the visitors against the local blacksmith. Alloway tossed his curveball effectively for eight innings against the local team of bully boys. In the ninth inning the umpire, upon advice from the blacksmith, forfeited the game to the hometown boys because "the pitcher has a crooked eye and throws a crooked ball." Then the locals chased the visitors out of town.

Who threw the first curveball? Fred Goldsmith died in 1939 with newspaper clippings crediting him with the invention of the curveball. He made the first public demonstration of the pitch on August 16, 1870.

Another claimant was Bobby Mathews. The *Cincinnati Enquirer* sponsored a contest and challenge during the 1877 season. Local physics professors set up two posts. Pitchers were asked to throw the ball on the left side of the near post and curve it around the right side of the far post. Reds hurler Bobby Mathews (3-12 that season) volunteered for the project. He curved the ball around the stakes almost every time. University of Cincinnati professors, who witnessed the exhibition, declared that a baseball cannot curve; it must have been an optical illusion. Despite the opposition from academia, the Baseball Hall of Fame recognized the curveball as a significant enough achievement to induct the man that sportswriters chose as the inventor of the pitch.

Arthur "Candy" Cummings is another contender. Cummings maintained that he got the idea for the curveball by watching the flight of clam shells that he threw on a New England beach as a 14 year old. His testimony, published in 1908, "How I pitched the First Curve," won the support of Henry Chadwick and the rest of the baseball establishment. Cummings was touted among the pioneers chosen for the Hall of Fame in 1939 as the inventor of the curveball. Not only a ballplayer, he helped to found the International Association and served as its chief executive, and he pitched in the 1877 league.

The First Relief Pitcher
Fireman on the Mound

1908

Bill James, in his landmark *Historical Baseball Abstract*, detailed the development of relief pitching. The first recognizable relief pitcher was Doc Crandall, who played from 1908 to 1918, including three trips to the World Series with the Giants. He was a strong hitter and a junk-ball pitcher. His relief appearances were mainly in middle relief, but he did start effectively as well as mop-up in relief.

Firpo Marberry (nicknamed after Luis Firpo, the Wild Bull of the Pampas who knocked Jack Dempsey out of the ring) was the first pitcher to be used primarily in relief. Bill James claimed that between 1924 and 1934 Marberry was as valuable as any pitcher in baseball except Lefty Grove. He had a career winning percentage of .623 without pitching for the Yankees or Athletics, the two best teams of his league.

Johnny Murphy, the Yankee reliever, 1934-43, was the first to be used as a regular reliever, not in a mop-up role. Another Yankee, Joe Page was the first to be used 50 to 60 times a season in important situations. Not only were Page and Hugh Casey, the giant flame thrower for the Brooklyn Dodgers, valuable members of their staffs, but they were key performers. Other teams during the 1950s saw the successes of the Yankees and Dodgers and rushed to acquire a relief specialist.

The reliever became an integral part of the baseball team during the second half of the twentieth century, and the rewards showed it. Jim Konstanty of the 1950 Phillies won the National League MVP Award. Larry Sherry of the Dodgers was the 1959 World Series MVP. Rollie Fingers led two teams, the Athletics and Brewers, into the World Series. Relievers who have won the Cy Young Award include Mike Marshall (1974), Sparky Lyle (1977), Bruce Sutter (1979), Rollie Fingers (1981), Willie Hernandez (1984), Steve Bedrosian (1987), Mark Davis (1989) and Dennis Eckersley (1992).

The First Cy Young Award Winner
Who was Cy Young?

1956

ABOVE: A young Don Drysdale (left) holds Don Newcombe's 1956 Cy Young Award — the first ever — as Newk shows off his NL MVP plaque. The small trophy in the middle is Drysdale's Dodger Rookie of the Year Award.

RIGHT: All-time wins leader Cy Young always reported to spring training in top condition as the result of spending his winters plowing the fields of his Ohio farm.

An interesting question, who was Cy Young and why was an award named after him? Denton True Young was an Ohio farm boy who won more games than the average baseball fan will see. Among his 511 victories were 76 shutouts and three no-hitters (one was perfect). In addition, old Cy (short for cyclone) started 815 games, finished 749 of them, and hurled 7,356 innings while striking out 2,803 and walking only 1,217. His 22-year career ended in 1911.

The award was established in 1955 (first awarded in 1956) because pitchers seldom drew votes in the MVP balloting. The immortal Young had died the previous year. The first recipient was Big Don Newcombe, who edged out Dodger teammate Sal "The Barber" Maglie. Only future Hall of Fame members Whitey Ford and Warren Spahn drew votes as electors were limited to one vote per team. Ironically, Newcombe also won the NL MVP Award, as the pitchers finally received their own recognition as well.

The Cy Young Award became an important incentive clause in player contract negotiations. A pitcher may earn $50,000 for the Cy Young Award, but the field tends to be dominated by a few good pitchers.

Three hurlers have captured four Cy Young awards: Steve Carlton, who intimidated National League batters and newspapermen; Roger Clemens, who added his fourth in 1997 11 years after he won his first; and Greg Maddux, whose closest competition came from his teammates.

The First Player Caught Doctoring the Baseball

No Cutting, No Splitting, No Boarding

1882

Indicative of earlier times when the baseball was subject to various manipulations, wily Burleigh Grimes prepares a legal spitball. Designated in 1920 as a spitballer, Grimes continued until he became the last legitimate practitioner of the pitch.

The pitcher was caught cutting the ball. On June 6, 1882, ex-pitcher Blondie Purcell, who was better known for using peroxide, was fined $10 for slicing the cover of a soggy ball, trying to get the new ball into the game. It seemed that his pitcher James "Pud" Galvin couldn't curve the old one, so he talked a teammate into doing his dirty work. He wasn't the last, nor the first, hurler to be accused of skullduggery.

Investigation and accusations of cheating in the pitcher's box began with the first star pitcher who got batters out consistently. Jim Creighton was investigated, watched and interrogated while proving his delivery legal. Even the curveball was frowned upon as cheating because the pitch fooled batters, even though the essence of pitching is to fool the batters. Sometimes, a pitcher used illegal means.

Prior to 1920, pitchers tossed legal spitballs, emery balls and shine balls (paraffin). After that date, because of a player's death after getting beaned, trick pitches using applied foreign substances were outlawed. Only 17 designated hurlers were allowed to continue using the spitball within the white major leagues, but the Negro Leagues still harbored an assortment of spitball and emery board pitchers. However, the list of those accused of tossing illegal pitches never seemed to end.

Fans who saw Gaylord Perry — caught and suspended in 1982 — late in his career remembered his faked grease ball on every pitch. In reality, he claimed to throw only four or five a game, but drove the opposition crazy waiting for them. Preacher Roe and Hugh Casey sometimes threw the "Cuban" forkball, as did Cubanos Pedro Ramos and Camilio Pascual. Several sources explained how Whitey Ford got extra movement on critical pitches with a studded wedding ring and the aid of ex-Negro League catcher Elston Howard. Lew Burdette, Phil Regan and Don Drysdale occasionally tossed a slippery pitch or two. Rick Rhoden and Mike Scott were vilified for throwing baseballs that happened to be scuffed on exactly the same spot, but they were never trapped as were two pitchers in 1987.

Joe Niekro of the Twins threw a slider that darted downward past Brian Downing at the plate. The home umpire went to the mound and asked Niekro to empty his pockets. Out fell an emery board and sandpaper. Not long afterward, Kevin Gross was caught with sandpaper on the mound. Both hurlers faced 10-day suspensions, the first since Rick Honeycutt's thumbtack in the glove got 10 days in 1980.

Managers

Compliments of BAUM & BERNSTEIN, Clothiers.

BROOKLYN

181.
Dave Foutz

Newsboy

NEW YORK.

The First Manager to use Cut-off Plays
One More Out

1893

David Foutz was more than a career .690 pitcher (tying Whitey Ford for second place on the all-time list), he was an innovator as a manager and on the playing field.

David L. Foutz, a pitcher, outfielder and manager with St. Louis and Brooklyn, packed a lot of pitching wins and batting hits into his prematurely shortened career. He won 41 games for the pennant-winning St. Louis Browns in the American Association in 1886. He batted .393 in 1887, the year walks counted as hits and batters feasted with four strikes instead of three. Foutz also won 25 games that year for another pennant winner. His hurling ability got him sold to Brooklyn, but his hitting kept him in the lineup at first base and outfield. It was at those two positions where Foutz developed his theory of cut-off plays. He reasoned that the cut-off play was really a reverse relay throw. The shortstop had been helping with relays since the 1850s. Foutz trained his Brooklyn team, where he managed 1893-96, to utilize a designated relay person in the infield. The first baseman or pitcher served to cutoff throws, catching runners trying to advance a base on an outfield throw. The cut-off concept slowed the aggressive baserunners of the 1890s and gave the defense one more method for making an out. Foutz died unexpectedly in the spring of 1897, cutting short a brilliant career.

The First Manager to
Practice Fielding Plays
Do it My Way

1868

Harry Wright, on the Philadelphia Phillies' bench, brought order and structure early on to the child's game of baseball. Under his guidance baseball became an adult pastime. He first devised fielding practice in the 1860s.

Harry Wright was born to play professional sports. His father was a paid cricketer. Harry went to Cincinnati as a cricket professional. There he became a $1,500-a-year bowler (cricket) and a semi-pro pitcher (baseball) with a wicked change of pace. In 1868, the Cincinnati Base Ball Club hired him to find "the best men procurable." He formed the professional Red Stockings. He also trained them through a series of fielding drills. Infield practice might seem mundane today, but in the 1860s it was revolutionary.

When the Red Stockings reverted to an amateur club following defeats in 1870, Harry and several team members moved to Boston, where they fielded a top-notch club called the Red Stockings. Harry's Reds responded to his teachings about practice and training by winning four pennants in five years. Over that period his Boston team went 225-60 for a .789 winning percentage. Two of his Red Stockings (Cincinnati and Boston) utilized his methods to become pennant-winning managers themselves, brother George with Providence and Albert Spalding with Chicago. Cap Anson, through Spalding, continued the idea of practice.

The First Manager to Endorse Nutrient Drinks

Magic Potions

1882

Managers are natural leaders of men. They have often felt that they can lead in commercial fields as well as on baseball diamonds. John McGraw of the New York Giants had won 10 National League pennants when he invited New Yorkers to invest in Florida real estate. The tract was known as Pennant Park with streets such as Mathewson Boulevard, Bresnahan Drive and Youngs Road. Tropical storms ravaged the area and all investors lost their shirts and life savings. Buyer beware when the endorser is a big league manager.

Ted Williams hawked Sears sporting goods, but only after he tested them. Tommy Lasorda endorsed SlimFast after he used it to lose many pounds from bon vivant, gourmand days. The Dodger skipper was not the first to endorse nutrient drinks.

Charles Comiskey, future owner of the Chicago White Sox, used a secret weapon to win four straight pennants during the

1880s with the St. Louis Browns. While other teams discussed the rule book and hit-and-run plays, the Brownies were tanking up on Comiskey's secret clubhouse nutrient drink. The ingredients were unknown, but it was potent enough to run the Brownies roughshod over the opposition. Whatever the secret was, it died with Comiskey's Browns and White Sox.

The First Manager to Win Five Straight World Series

The Ol' Perfessor

1953

Casey Stengel (in the middle) celebrates his first Yankee pennant after a thrilling 5–3 win over the Boston Red Sox on the last day of the 1949 season, the year he skippered the Bombers to the first of five straight World Championships.

The Yankees stocked the top farm system and hired the best front office people for decades. General managers Edward Barrow and George Weiss plus president Larry MacPhail traveled from the Yankee office to the Hall of Fame. No matter how much money or how good the material in the farm system, the Bombers still need a manager. The man who assessed the talent and made the right moves on the playing field during the 1950s was Casey Stengel, who as a player had stayed with and cooked breakfast for Giants manager John McGraw and his wife at spring training in Florida in the 1920's. McGraw and Stengel had talked baseball, day and night. Casey learned a valuable lesson in platoon baseball when he hit .368 and .339 as a platoon outfielder under McGraw.

As a manager, Stengel used the platoons at third base — Dr. Bobby Brown and Billy Johnson — and in left field with Hank Bauer and Gene Woodling, to win five straight American League pennants and five straight World Series titles, 1949-53. Until Casey, no manager had ever won five straight World Champion-ships or used as many players. No manager had ever won nine flags in ten years, but Casey did.

The First Manager to Use a Lefty/Righty Relief Combo

Platoon on the Mound

1972

Dick Williams has Hall of Fame credentials. While innovating platooning pitchers, he won pennants in both leagues — Boston and Oakland in the AL and San Diego in the NL — and captured back-to-back World Championships with the A's.

The players on the Oakland A's won three straight pennants and World Series titles, 1972-74, despite the meddling of owner Charles Finley, who openly feuded with players, managers, the press and everybody else. He clashed with Commissioner Bowie Kuhn over the sale of Vida Blue and Rollie Fingers to the Yankees. Kuhn voided the deal, claiming it destroyed baseball's competitive balance. Finley, who once called Kuhn "the village idiot," said he would lose the players to free agency if he didn't sell them. He lost them, but no owner cared. Kuhn also clashed with Finley during the 1973 World Series when the A's owner tried to "fire" second baseman Mike Andrews, who was in a batting slump, by placing him on the disabled list. The team was livid with rebellion as the commissioner overruled Finley's act. How did the A's win?

Oakland went to war with their near-genius manager, Dick Williams. Baltimore's Earl Weaver was elected to the Hall of Fame, yet Williams had more wins, more World Series titles and trailed Weaver by one pennant, four to three. An underrated skipper, Williams introduced the concept of lefty/right relievers out of the bullpen. The effect befuddled rival managers. Williams negated the platoon advantage and turned the final innings of a ball game into a war of attrition. Williams used left-handers Paul Lindblad and Darryl Knowles with righties Rollie Fingers, Horacio Pina, Bob Locker and Blue Moon Odom out of the pen to overwhelm American League opponents.

The First Manager Ejected from a World Series Game

Timeout, per Chance

1910

BELOW LEFT: Future Hall of Fame umpire Tommy Connolly ejected Manager Chance during the 1910 World Series.

BELOW RIGHT: Frank Chance used his fists as well as his brain to impose discipline and leadership on the 1900s Chicago Cubs.

When illness forced Manager Frank Selee's temporary retirement in 1905, burly Frank Chance was named leader of the Cubs. The team was beset by personnel problems. The second baseman and shortstop did not speak to each other. The catcher was so upset with the anti-Semitic attitudes of his teammates and fans that he walked off the team in 1909 — the only year from 1906 to 1910 that the Cubs did not win the pennant. The third baseman felt slighted because he was not heralded in the poem "Tinker to Evers to Chance" as were the other members of the infield. The center fielder — and his family — felt that he was the catalyst and star player on the team that won four pennants in five years.

Chance, called Husk because of his physical build and aggressive stance, ruled the Cubs with iron fists. He never backed down, and enforced discipline among the Cubs with determined resolution. The result was a talented, determined squad that won 66 percent of their games in the seven years that Chance managed them. Seldom riled and usually calm, even amidst the turmoil that surrounded the Giants' John McGraw and the Pirates' Barney Dreyfus, Chance blew his cool one afternoon in the 1910 World Series.

Trailing two game to none versus the young and brash Philadelphia A's, the Cubs felt old. Connie Mack's kids had run and bunted the proud Cubs into submission. Before Game One, Chance had had a tremendous argument with the American League umpire Tommy Connally about movie cameras on the playing field and behind home plate. The start of the World Series had been delayed 30 minutes while National Leaguers Chance and umpire Hank O'Day ordered film makers from the field. Instead of going quietly they marched straight to the box of American League President Ban Johnson, who had given them permission to film the Series. Chance and the National League lost as the cinematographers stayed. Chance brooded in a black mood. The third game, in Chicago, was sorely needed if the Cubs were going to escape this ambush set by Mack and the American League.

The overflow crowd necessitated special ground rules. Balls hit into the crowd scored as ground-rule doubles. With the score tied 3-3 in the top of the third, the Athletics exploded for five runs, the highlight being a controversial home run by Danny Murphy, whose drive hit high on the right-field fence. American League umpire Tommy Connally ruled that the portion of the fence hit by Murphy's drive was free of spectators, therefore a home run and not a ground rule double. Chance came unglued. He argued, "When is a ground rule not a ground rule?" He kicked long enough and loud enough to be removed from the game, becoming the first manager ever removed from a World Series game.

The First African-American Manager
I'll Show You How

1975

Cleveland's Frank
Robinson shakes hands
with Commissioner Bowie
Kuhn on Opening Day
1975 before his historic
first game as the Indians'
player-manager.

n the 25 years following Jackie Robinson's debut in 1947, major league baseball clubs had farm teams that played 3,491 seasons (teams times seasons). In that time, exactly three black men — Sam Bankhead (one year), Gene Banks (two years) and Hector Lopez (one year) — managed minor league teams for a combined four years.

When Frank Robinson was offered the player/manager job for Cleveland, he became the first African-American to manage a baseball team in the history of the major leagues. In his first game, Opening Day, April 8, 1975, Manager Robinson batted DH Robinson second in the lineup. On his first at-bat Robinson showed his old style. He pulled a low and away fastball from Doc Medich into the left-field stands. It was his eighth Opening Day home run, tying the record. The home run amazed fans and teammates. He hit on cue like he did in 1966 when the Cincinnati general manager had traded him to Baltimore, saying that he was "an old 30." Robinson had responded with his best season as he led the American League in batting average, home runs and RBI, winning the Triple Crown.

Umpires and Officials

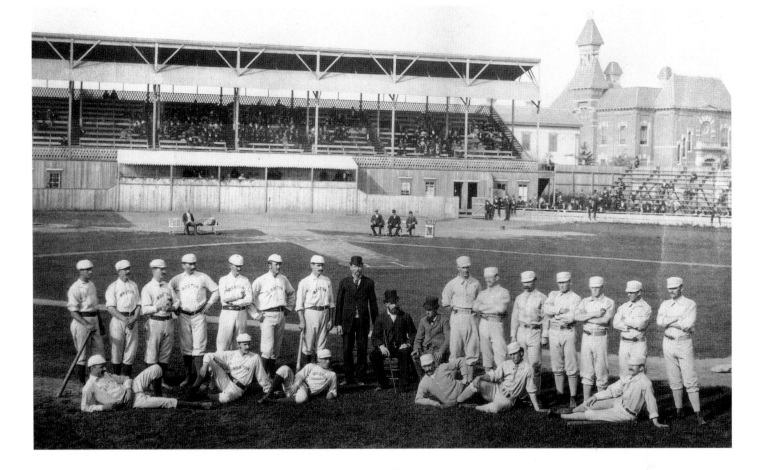

The First Umpire Staff

And Justice for All

1879

The 1879 Boston and Providence clubs benefited from the first professional umpire staff. The two teams, pictured here, were managed by the Wright brothers, Harry with Boston and George in a Providence uniform.

I n 1879 the National League introduced a staff of 20 umpires who were located in the different cities of the league. Captains were free to choose among the designated hometown umpires, but such arrangements caused trouble. Too often, umpires felt it was their civic duty to rule in favor of the home team. Umpires were paid $5.00 per game, with no money for transportation or food. This first home-based staff included Charles Daniels, Billy McLean, Mike Walsh, James Summer, W.E. Furlong, C. E. Wilbur, A. D. Hodges, George Seward, James A. Williams, William H. Geer, J. Dunn, J. A. Cross, R. Wheeler, G. W. Bredburg, Charles G. Stambaugh, T. H. Brunton, T. Gilliam, F. W. Feber, J. Young and E. G. Fountain. The home-based umpires knew the rules, had experience and guaranteed that they would show up, but their fairness was suspect.

What was needed was an independent source of umpires. The American Association, at its founding (1882) created a paid, full staff of umpires. For the magnificent sum of $140 per month plus $3.00 per day for travel and food, the league office delivered a professional umpire staff to its member clubs. Umpires could levy $25 fines for profanity, but were prohibited from borrowing money from players or club officials. The following year the National League copied what was a good idea from the American Association by establishing its own set of professional staff umpires without hometown biases.

The First Umpire to Use
an Inside Chest Protector
Catfish

1908

Usually chosen to umpire
the crucial National League
games during the early
1900s, Bill Klem was cool
before large, hostile
crowds. He also innovated
the inside chest protector.

"Baseball to me is not a game, it is a religion," declared
National League umpire Bill Klem. Generally recognized
as the best umpire ever to call a game, Klem — also
known as Catfish — was so highly regarded that he
umpired exclusively behind the plate for the first 16 years of
his National League career. There he discovered the value of
an inside chest protector. Prior to Klem's appearance with the
inside pad, umpires wore the "balloon" outside. Klem felt that his
vision was sometimes blocked by the bulkiness of the outside
protector. He took a catcher's chest protector, added shoulder
pads and wore it under his shirt. Because of his prominence,
National League arbitrators adopted the inside style while the
Junior League counterparts continued the outside pad until the
1960s. The difference was always most noticeable during the
World Series.

Klem was a fixture at the annual Fall Classic. He officiated
at 18 of them, starting in 1908 and ending with the 1940 Reds–
Tigers battle. After that he served as chief of National League
umpires. He always maintained that he never called one wrong,
though later in life he added, "in my heart." So great was his
dedication to umpiring, Klem retired when he only "thought,"
but couldn't be sure, that a man had been tagged out.

The First Umpire to Use Hand Signals

Sign Language

1905

BELOW RIGHT: Cy Rigler filled the right tackle slot for the original Massillon Tigers professional football team. He claimed to have originated hand signals while umpiring in the minor leagues in 1905.

FAR RIGHT: Deaf William "Dummy" Hoy, who claimed to have been the reason that umpires developed hand signals, threw out the first pitch for Game Three of the 1961 World Series.

The legend was that as a deaf-mute outfielder in the 1886-87 Northwest League, William Ellsworth Hoy, asked the umpire — there was only one in those days — to gesture with his hands whether a baserunner was out or safe. The simple signs, hands outstretched with palms down for safe and a jerk of the thumb for out, became popular with the players and fans. For sure, National League arbitrator Bill Klem was one of the first in the Senior Circuit to add emphatic arm gestures for calls to his repertoire.

The hulking Cy Rigler began his umpiring career in the 1905 minor leagues. There he claimed to have originated the raised right hand for called strikes. Whatever the origin, the hand gestures were well received by player and fan alike.

The First Umpire to Write a Book
Most Valuable Umpire

1912

Billy Evans earned respect and admiration for the AL umpiring staff when his syndicated national column about umpiring began to appear in the 1920s. Evans' many talents led him to be selected to the Baseball Hall of Fame in 1973.

Brought up from Class C to the American League in 1906 by Ban Johnson, college-educated William G. "Billy" Evans, at age 22, became the youngest umpire in major league history, and the only one to make the jump straight from Class C to the majors. The multi-talented Evans wrote a syndicated column, *Billy Evans Says*, and a book, *Umpiring from the Inside*. He gave up the indicator and broom in 1927 for a job with the Cleveland Indians as general manager. He was the first baseball executive to hold that title. Besides being a swell dresser and front office executive, Evans once fought Ty Cobb under the stands after a baseball game.

Al Schacht described the fight in his book *Clown Prince*. "When the game ended they both went under the grandstand while the members of both teams became spectators. Billy posed like a real fighter while Ty stalked him like a Tiger and then suddenly hit him in the jaw. Down went Evans with Ty on top of him. With his knee on Evans' chest, Ty held Billy by the throat and tried to choke him. We finally got him off Billy and that was the end of the fight." As a result, Cobb was banned for life from the American League, but no one paid attention as Cobb and the other baseball stars retired to join U.S. troops in the first World War. When the war was over, Cobb came back and his banishment was forgotten by all except Billy Evans.

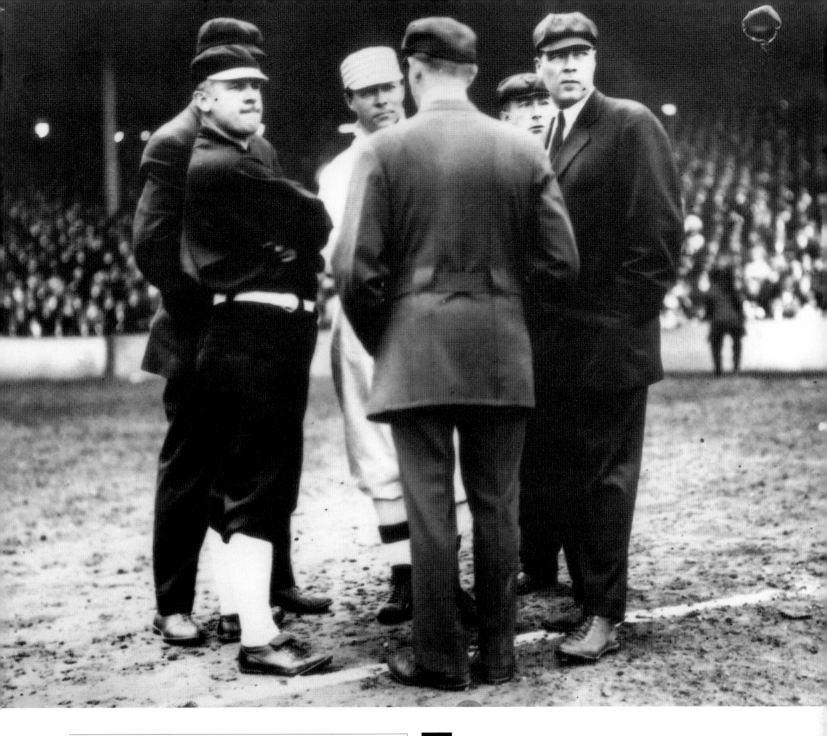

The First Umpire to Eject a Player
Who Dun It??

Managers and umpires confer during the 1911 World Series. Contending with hostile fans and intransigent players during baseball's early days, umpires resorted to ejections and fines and, if all else failed, the rule of might.

The name of the umpire who called the June 19, 1846, game (long celebrated as the first game) between the Knickerbockers and the New York nine has been lost to history, but the player he fined was well-known. James Whyte Davis (who was later buried in his baseball uniform) of the Knickerbockers was fined six cents for swearing, in accordance with the new club constitution. The umpire may have been William R. Wheaton, whom the Knickerbocker club had appointed. He officiated at an earlier recorded game on October 6, 1845. If he tossed any player, it was not recorded.

Who then, was the first player ejected by an umpire? Certainly by the 1890s, intimidation had become the rule rather than the exception. Some umpires fought back. Ex-prize fighter Billy McLean offered to fight the toughest guy in the stands. Others umps pulled weapons on unruly crowds. Still others sought protection from the ball teams, who never failed to support the arbitrator in his time of need. At least, that was true on the major league level. Players and police used ball, bats and lead batons several times to open paths through unruly mobs for the umpires to retreat to the clubhouse.

The First Umpire to Throw a Game
A Crooked Tale

1882

The 1882 Detroit
Wolverines, posing in the
color-coded by position
uniforms, played a role
in discovering the deceit
by arbiter Dick Higham.
Famed promoter and man-
ager Frank Bancroft is seated in the middle.

Players have been suspended and kicked out of baseball. Owners have been disciplined and suspended, even expelled for betting, but only one solitary umpire has ever been accused of crookedness. The first and only betting scandal involving an umpire was uncovered by the Detroit team president, William G. Thompson, in 1882. The England-born Richard Higham authored an incriminating letter that told gamblers how to bet on games that he officiated. The renegade ump was barred from baseball for life. It was not Higham's first brush with crookedness. As a player with the Syracuse Stars in 1877, he and his teammates had participated in two three-team tournaments that ended in draws. Fans in Pittsburgh and Milwaukee left the ballparks feeling that the Stars had allowed the tied tournaments.

The 1882 umpire scandal led directly to the National League hiring a full-time, paid staff in the same manner as the American Association. Umpires never again were caught trying to sell a game. They established their own code of behavior and deported themselves with dignity during the trying times of the nineteenth century. Arbitrators got a break when Ban Johnson founded the American League on the principle of respecting the umpire, the official in charge of the game. It took the National League several more years to understand the concept. Finally, as the best players from the Senior Circuit jumped or drifted to the new league, the old magnates realized that fans did not attend games to harass the umpire or see the umpire harassed, they wanted to see a well-played game of baseball.

The First Commissioner of Baseball
Mr. Baseball

1921

The first commissioner of baseball, Judge Kenesaw Mountain Landis ruled baseball with an iron fist from 1921 until his death in December 1944.

The possibility loomed that the champion White Sox might win the 1920 American League pennant, but their regulars would be suspended for participation in the 1919 Black Sox scandal. The starters would have had to use "get out of jail free" cards to play in the World Series. This was a problem for baseball. "We need a czar" became the cry of the owners. The recently overthrown Russian autocrat represented to the western world and baseball's upper echelon absolute power. The owners selected a federal judge, Kenesaw Mountain Landis, who swore to remove gambling dens, stop the selling of games, prohibit association with known gamblers, and generally look out for the best interests of baseball. The owners got more than they bargained for. In Judge Landis they found a czar. He barred the eight Black Sox from baseball for life.

But Judge Landis' appointment did not come easily. The Judge wanted control of the minors as well as the majors. The National Association met long hours and exchanged dozens of telegrams trying to convince the minor leagues to get on the band wagon. When the Association finally agreed to limited control by the new office of commissioner of baseball, Landis signed, on January 21, 1921. He stayed until his death in 1944. His iron-fisted rule held owners and players alike in check. He became known as a fans' advocate.

Subsequent commissioners have struggled to live up to the example set by Landis. He was both fair and arbitrary, twice releasing from reserved status dozens of farm hands. Each succeeding commissioner brought strengths and weaknesses to the job, but saw their influence eroded until, by the 1980s, the power of the position had dissolved.

The First Players' Union
Players Unite!

1885

RIGHT: Timothy Keefe won 342 games in 14 years and served as an executive in the first players' union.
BELOW LEFT: John Clarkson, who won 328 games in a career that ranged from 1882 to 1894, battled against management in 1887.
BELOW RIGHT: John Montgomery Ward formed the first players' union, leading to the great Player Rebellion of 1890. Later he became a successful attorney in Brooklyn.

When John Clarkson was sold to Pittsburgh in 1887 he refused to report unless he was given half of the purchase price. Other ballplayers asked each other, "How is this possible? How can we be sold as slaves, when the Constitution outlawed slavery?" Suddenly, John Montgomery Ward's complaints about the player contract hit home.

Since 1885, the founding year of the first players' union, called the Brotherhood, Ward and his brother-in-law Timothy Keefe had complained about inequity in baseball. The earliest goals of the Brotherhood were the writing of players' full salaries into the contracts, correcting abuses of the suspension list, and having a voice in the affairs of the league and clubs. In the Clarkson instance, he was not sold, but his contract was. The first union had trouble with the owners who, at first, refused to recognize it. In time, the union's negotiating demands moved past written salaries to the abolition of reserving players at a lower salary. The owners were against the players' demands because they cost money and they meant sharing power with the players.

For decades after 1885, player unions lacked full-time employees and permanent locations. In 1966, the Major League Baseball Players Association (MLBPA) selected Marvin Miller, a steel workers union official, as its full-time Executive Director. His first success was to wrangle a better contract from Topps Baseball Card Company. He next established a licensing program that became worth millions of dollars. He forced the owners to accept the MLBPA as the players' bargaining agent, while fashioning a written contract between the players and owners. The Players' Union survived several strikes, lockouts and work stoppages to emerge as the most powerful and influential body in unionism today.

LEFT: Marvin Miller, Wes Parker (partially obscured) and Joe Torre announce to the baseball writers the end of the 1972 13-day player strike.

BELOW: Donald Fehr, Marvin Miller and Richard Moss (l to r) celebrate the 25th anniversary of the Major League Baseball Players Association with the publication of Miller's autobiography, *A Whole New Ball Game,* in 1991.

Firsts

The First African-Americans in Professional Baseball
Moses, Welday and Bud

1884

Jackie Robinson, in a Montreal Royals uniform in 1946, walloped four hits, three singles and a home run, in the first Organized Baseball contest played by a recognized black man in the twentieth century. It was a startling debut, but it accomplished much more. It showed what a Negro League player could do, if given the opportunity. It proved equality in direct competition against white professional players. Robinson's minor league debut made his major league entry, next year, a foregone conclusion and an eagerly anticipated event. But he wasn't the first.

Oberlin graduates Moses Fleetwood Walker and Welday Walker used professional baseball to pay their bills. The two roomed together on the Toledo Blue Stockings of the 1883 Northwest League. When their club was accepted for membership in the expanding American Association, the two black brothers accompanied their squad to the big leagues. Though neither tore the league apart, they made a significant impact on race relations as Moses toiled many more years in the high minors and Welday went into publishing. Even better known than the Walkers was Bud Fowler.

Fowler starred for more than 20 years, including 10 in white integrated leagues. As a young pitcher he defeated the NL's Boston club in an 1878 exhibition game. He played for 17 teams in nine leagues, seldom batting less than .300 for a season. He also operated a barbershop in Cooperstown, New York, near the current site of the Baseball Hall of Fame. Fowler barnstormed and started the Page Fence Giants before giving up their road career to return to Organized Ball.

RIGHT: Bill Veeck, owner of the Cleveland Indians, signed Larry Doby to a big league contract. Doby then became the American League's first African-American player almost three months after Robinson started with the Dodgers.

BELOW: Jackie Robinson, normally a middle infielder, converted to a first baseman for the 1947 season. For his play that year, Robinson was selected as the first Rookie of the Year.

The First Latin Ballplayer
The Beat Goes On

1871

Roberto Clemente may not have been the first Latin ballplayer, but he was the first superstar from the Caribbean area, and his achievements opened doors for others. He became known simply as "The Great One."

The first Latin major league player was Estaban Bellan. He starred for the Troy Haymakers at the beginning of the old National Association. He returned to Cuba after eight games with the New York Mutuals in 1873. Back in Cuba he was the driving force behind the Cuban professional league, which held its first tournament in 1878. Bellan and Emilio Sourbin, organizer of the Havana ball club, promoted and proselytized for the sport until Sourbin ran afoul of Spanish authorities and was imprisoned, baseball being banned in parts of the colony. The importation of Latin ballplayers into the majors would wait until the turn of the century.

Colombia's Luis Castro played part of the 1902 season for Connie Mack's A's, and two light-skinned Cubans, Armando Marsans and Rafael Almeida, brought Caribbean influence back to major league baseball when they signed with Cincinnati in 1911. Several more light-skinned Latinos, including Dolf Luque, played for the Long Branch Cubans in the New York-New Jersey minor league around the same time. At this time only half of the Latin population was eligible to play in the majors.

When Jackie Robinson broke the self-imposed color line of Major League Baseball, he did more than blaze a path for African-Americans. He led the way for ballplayers of all colors to integrate the majors. Many black Latinos had been barred for playing in the big leagues. The Caribbean area has produced numerous star players including Roberto Clemente, and more recently Sammy Sosa, Juan Gonzalez, Pudge Rodriguez, Carlos Delgado, Wil Cordero and Jose Offerman.

The First Gambling Scandal in Pro Ball

Take the Money for a Run

1877

TOP: The "Black Sox" World Series fix, while not pro ball's first scandal, became its most well-known. In this 1919 Chicago White Sox photo, Joe Jackson is in the top row, second from right.
BOTTOM: The *New York Times* headline tells the rest of the story.

n the 1877 pennant race Boston overtook Louisville, who inexplicably lost every game on a late-season eastern road trip, and the National League was faced with its first professional betting scandal. Four players on the Louisville club were presented with evidence of a plot to throw games. Three of the guilty four confessed to the scheme. All were suspended from baseball for life and never allowed to return. The swiftness and finality of baseball justice influenced Judge Kenesaw Mountain Landis when he later ruled on the eligibility of the Black Sox.

The "Dirty Linen" from the 1919 World Series was aired publicly at the Grand Jury investigation during September 1920. The White Sox players had knowingly agreed to throw the 1919 Series in exchange for the promise of money. They were angry with White Sox owner Charles Comiskey, who had promised them bonuses for winning the 1917 World Series, but had never paid them. Also, Comiskey was thought to have ordered pitcher Ed Cicotte rested to prevent him from collecting a bonus for winning 30 games. Furthermore, the players resented the manner in which Comiskey flaunted his wealth. The affluent White Sox owner hosted groups of sportswriters and sportsmen — the Woodland Bards — to outings and repasts in the Michigan woods. The players sought revenge for alleged wrongs and they thought they had achieved it by losing the 1919 World Series. The players and fans never thought that anything bad would happen to them.

Judge Landis sought in one mighty blow to end such practices. His banning of the Chicago Eight, despite their acquittal by a Chicago jury, sent icy shivers down the spines of every player who had a slight twinge of dishonesty. Landis' actions were heeded by later commissioners Bart Giamatti and Faye Vincent in their dealings with Pete Rose, baseball's all-time hit leader, who was banned from baseball in 1989 for gambling involvement while managing the Reds.

The First Player to Win
a League MVP Award
The Envelope, Please

1911

Ty Cobb, in the automobile on the right, drives Hugh Chalmers of the Chalmers Automobile Company around the ballpark after having won the car in the 1910 batting race. Due to controversy in scorekeeping, the other batting champ contender, Nap Lajoie, was presented with a car as well (left).

Prior to the 1910 season Hugh Chalmers, president and general manager of the Chalmers Motor Company, announced that he would present one of his company's automobiles, a Chalmers 30, to the major league player who compiled the highest batting average. What started as a promotional gimmick turned into the greatest controversy in baseball history.

The batting race developed into a two-man affair, Ty Cobb of Detroit and Nap Lajoie of Cleveland, both American Leaguers. Throughout the season there were charges and counter-charges of favoritism by scorers in various cities. Furthermore, the consensus of the press was that Cobb's selfish pursuit of this individual honor had cost his team the pennant. The batting race was capped by a scandalous circumstance on the final day of the season.

Both hitters blistered September pitching, Cobb at .532 and Lajoie at .556. Cobb sat out the final day, thinking that he had an insurmountable lead, though due to poor record keeping no one knew the real averages. While Cobb sat, Lajoie played a doubleheader and went 8-for-8 with seven bunts. The rookie third sacker Red Corriden was ordered to play back by Browns manager Jack O'Connor, allowing the bunts to become hits. American League President Ban Johnson investigated and announced that he had found a discrepancy and that Cobb was the real winner. Chalmers gave automobiles to both players. Society for American Baseball Research and Hall of Fame studies 70 years later showed additional mistakes in Cobb's and Lajoie's batting records for that year, but Cobb still won the 1910 batting title.

The next year a Chalmers automobile was given to the player in each league who "should prove himself as the most important and useful player to his club and to the league at large in point of deportment and value of services rendered." The recipient would be chosen by a panel of sportswriters, one from each club in each league. The voters balloted eight names which would receive weight votes, eight for first place, seven for second and so forth. The winners in 1911 were Ty Cobb (American League) and Frank Schulte of the Cubs (National League). Both players voluntarily took themselves out of the voting for 1912. The award quietly disappeared in 1914, but the idea survived to resurface in 1922.

The First Millionaire in Baseball

Business of Baseballs

1911

BELOW: In 1981 Nolan Ryan became the first to sign a $1 million contract. Ryan ended his career with the Rangers, where at age 40 his fastball was still clocked in the high 90s.

BELOW RIGHT: Young Al Spalding, whose main pitch was a change of pace, holds the ball and dreams of the sports empire that would make him baseball's first millionaire.

During the 1950s television watchers stared wide-eyed at the show *The Millionaire*. The premise of the program illustrated the element of luck in securing fortune. John Beresford Tipton started each telecast by opening a phonebook and selecting at random the name of a person who would receive a cashier's check for $1 million. The rest of show would demonstrate how sudden wealth affected the recipient.

Back in the nineteenth century, players had to work for money. Albert Goodwell Spalding was likely the first ex-player to make $1 million. His sporting goods empire, started by his brother Walter while Al was still a player, stretched around the world. Spalding always bragged that every country visited by the baseball travelers during the famous 1888-89 world tour fought on the Allied side during World War I. He forgot to mention that Spalding established commercial outlets and ties in each of the countries as well.

The second millionaire player, Lena Blackburne, inherited $2 million from a dead uncle at age 25 in April 1911. He continued to play as a rather nondescript journeyman ballplayer. In fact, he had been sent back to the minors after batting .174 in 1910. After inheriting the pre-income tax money, he spent more than 20 years as a player, manager and coach. Then he discovered that mud from the Delaware River that flowed through his land had unique properties and could be processed to make it highly sought after as "rubbing mud" for umpires. His business flourished, and when he grew too old to slog through the river bottom, he sold the business to Burns Bintliff and his five sons, who have continued the secret mud harvesting tradition.

Another millionaire who played baseball was Mario Hernandez, 32-year-old president and principal stockholder of the Mexicali Aguilas. He played first base for his own Sunset League pennant-winning club in 1948. The Arizona-born entrepreneur hit .255 and drove in 74 runs in 103 games. The first player to sign a million dollar contract was Nolan Ryan, who made the deal with the Houston Astros in 1981. He started the ascension of salaries that has led to today's $70 million payrolls.

The First Player
to Become Professional
Paid to Play

1865

Albert Reach became the
first paid professional
ballplayer in 1865. Later,
he started a sporting goods
company that rivaled that
of the Spalding brothers.
Even though Reach and
Spalding joined their companies in 1893, they con-
tinued to operate them as
competitors.

The Albert Reach story was the story of Horatio Alger, the rags-to-riches dream of every American boy. Born in England in 1840, he was brought to America as an infant. As a poor boy in Brooklyn, he earned his first pennies peddling newspapers and later worked in an iron foundry. When he died, he was a captain of industry, reputedly worth millions of dollars.

Early in life, Reach was attracted to the game of baseball. Despite his small stature he soon became skilled enough to join the well-known Brooklyn Eckfords. While playing for the so-called amateur Eckfords he was offered $25 in expense money to join the Philadelphia Athletics. Some historians claim that Jim Creighton was the first paid player. He played for the Excelsiors in 1861 or '62, but he died before he could stake his claim. Albert Reach proclaimed to the fans and the baseball public that he was a paid professional ballplayer in 1865. Soon hundreds were clamoring to obtain a paid job for playing baseball.

Reach used his brains and contacts to form companies which manu-factured and marketed baseball equipment to the general public. One was the Reach Sporting Goods Company. He also started the *Reach Baseball Guide* in 1883, which was pub-lished annually until 1939.

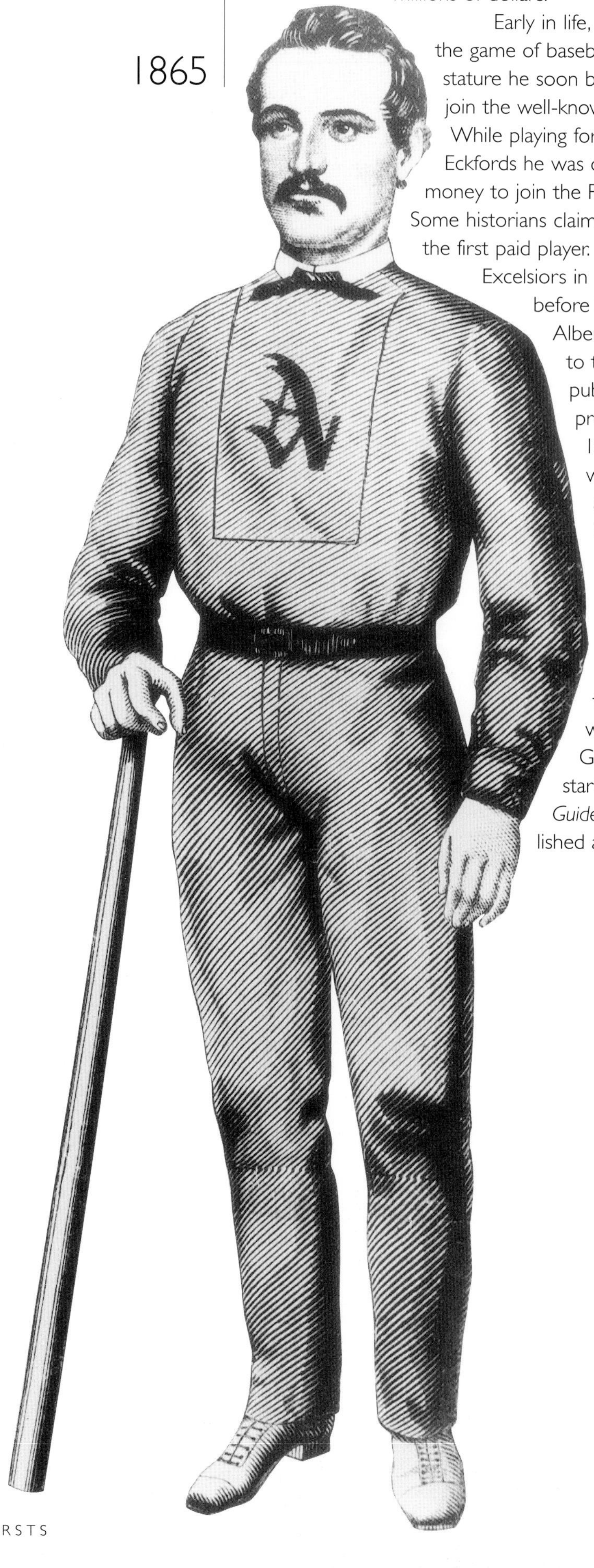

The First Player to Use His Name in a Business
Wright & Ditson

1870s

TOP: An early comer to bat making, Hillerich & Bradsbury began to produce the popular Louisville Slugger at the turn of the century. The company paid, over the years, millions for endorsements, but Pete Browning, the original "Louisville Slugger," received nothing and has yet to be elected the Baseball Hall of Fame.
RIGHT: Al Spalding rose from player to manager to renowned businessman to empire builder.

Peck and Snyder specialized in sporting goods before baseball became popular. To encourage interest in the budding baseball marketplace, they issued baseball cards, one per year, 1868-70.

Imagine the consternation when old-line Peck and Snyder discovered that George Wright, the brightest star in baseball and shortstop of the Boston Red Stockings, joined forces with a Boston businessman named Ditson to establish a rival sporting goods company. Wright started a move that would see Albert and Walter Spalding form a sporting goods company. Then Albert Reach started one with Ben Shibe as principle backer.

At the turn of the century star players sought endorsement and business opportunities, but they could not enter the sporting goods field because Spalding, Reach and Shibe dominated the ball, equipment and uniform markets. But bat making was different. Hillerich & Bradsbury produced the famed Louisville Slugger, although the Louisville club had been a chronic tail-end finisher and was dropped from the National League. Louisville needed to upgrade its image, so company officials spoke with Honus Wagner, a young star with the local team. He was persuaded to endorse the Louisville Slugger bat. Other players, seeing that Wagner received his money on time, became interested in a similar arrangement. Frank Chance followed Wagner at bat endorsement. Napoleon Lajoie endorsed chewing tobacco and even published his own baseball guide. By the eve of the First World War, ballplayers had obtained a sense of their worth in the business world.

The First Player to Hold Out for More Money

Show Me the Money

1870

Though not the first to hold out for more money, Edd Roush became the holdout champ in the 1920s. He was worth the price, as when he saved five runs with two amazing catches and scored crucial runs in the ill-fated 1919 World Series.

Charles Sweasy of Cincinnati held out in 1870 for 200 more dollars. Sweasy was a veteran ballplayer who had starred the previous season with the undefeated Red Stockings. He played with Cincinnati for the 1870 season, so presumably his demand had been met. Scotland-born Big Jim McCormick held out in 1887 for money from the sale of his contract to Pittsburgh. The Chicago White Stockings settled with their former player. Four years later Brotherhood union official Fred Pfeffer held out for more money and fewer fines. Pfeffer staged a sit-down strike in hometown Louisville until he was traded to Louisville.

Ty Cobb and Sam Crawford held out in 1914 in tandem. The pair of Tiger stars took advantage of the Federal League war to demand $20,000 for Cobb and a four-year contract for the 36-year-old Crawford. They both got what they wanted.

Hold out champ was Edd Roush, who sat out all or parts of 1922, 1927 and 1930. He routinely held out during spring training, demanding his full value. He was quoted by Hall of Fame historian Lee Allen, "I didn't hold out because I wanted to, but I never heard of any other method open to a ballplayer for getting the money." Even Babe Ruth, the highest-paid player, held out in 1928 spring training. He received $80,000 per annum for five years.

Dodger pitchers Sandy Koufax and Don Drysdale asked for a combination $1 million spread over three years. They took the audacious step of hiring a Hollywood agent, J. William Hayes, to represent them. Dodger owner Walter O'Malley — best known for moving the Dodgers from Brooklyn to Los Angeles — was outraged at the breach of baseball etiquette. He was quoted, "I never have discussed a player contract with an agent and I like to think I never will." Koufax and Drysdale got $240,000 a piece for their 32-day AWOL effort.

The First Crossover Football/Baseball

Extra Points

1895

BELOW: Ed Abbaticchio was the first baseball player to play pro football.
BELOW RIGHT: Jim Thorpe played baseball for the New York Giants and non-league pro football during the 1910s.

1898

The coal-mining area of Pennsylvania and Ohio produced football players in abundance. Not surprisingly, the first baseballers who played football came from that region. Giants pitcher Christy Mathewson (football in 1902) and outfielder George Barclay (football in 1897), both stars at Bucknell University, donned the togs of professional football, as did pitcher Rube Waddell. A Pittsburgh area pro team featured college backs — and big league baseball players — David Fultz (Brown), John Gammons (Brown) and Fred Crolius (Dartmouth) as star runners. But the first baseball player to play pro football was Ed Abbaticchio, who became known as the first punter to spiral a football. He played at Latrobe — home of golfing great Arnold Palmer — from 1895 through 1900. Early athletes were not only two-sport stars, but one even played three pro sports.

Ernie Nevers pitched for the Browns (he gave up home runs to Babe Ruth in 1927), scored 38 touchdowns and passed for 25 more in a five-year career with the Duluth Eskimos and Chicago Bears, and scored field goals in a Chicago-area pro basketball league. After Nevers, the triple-threat sports star existed only in books, but several very athletic players continued the double-sport tradition. The best of the two-sport athletes was Jim Thorpe, who passed his finest days in the uniforms of the baseball New York Giants and non-league pro football during the 1910s. By the time the National Football League (NFL) formed in 1920 Thorpe was over the hill in football and out of baseball. However, the NFL solicited two of its most influential men from baseball.

George Halas patrolled right field for the New York Yankees in 1919 before devoting his entire time to the Decatur Stanleys of the NFL. The Stanleys became the Chicago Bears. The other man was Joe Carr, the second president of the National Football League. Joseph Carr was president of the Ohio State baseball league and founder of the Columbus Panhandles football team. He also served three years as leader of the American Basketball Association, leaving in 1928 to become director of the promotion department of baseball's National Association. Under his tenure the minor leagues jumped from 12 leagues in 1933 to 41 in 1939 at his death. His fearlessness to employ multi-sport athletics carried through the twentieth century.

During the 1980s and 1990s Bo Jackson (Oakland Raiders and Kansas City Royals) and Deion Sanders (Atlanta Falcons, San Francisco 49ers, Dallas Cowboys and New York Yankees, Cincinnati Reds) thrilled sports fans. Both were extremely fast in both sports. Jackson retired to an injury sustained while running the football for the Oakland Raiders. He returned to baseball in 1993 with an artificial hip. He hit 29 home runs in two years,

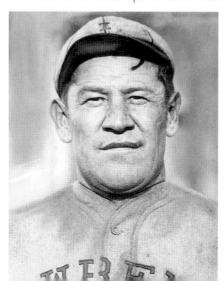

but the injury hampered him too much. Bo's counterpart Deion Sanders was a fast-talking, loose-playing football star, but a hard-working, nose-to-the-grindstone, team player on the baseball diamond. He led the National League in triples in 1992.

The First Player to Espouse a Chicken Diet

A Poultry Fortune

1871

Wade Boggs won four consecutive batting titles with the Red Sox in the 1980s. He played on five division winners and one World Championship team (Yankees in 1996). Boggs attributed much of his success to his chicken diet, as did little known Charles Pabor a century earlier.

Wade Boggs, star hitter for the Boston Red Sox and New York Yankees, who later played for the Tampa Bay Devil Rays, made headlines during the 1980s with an adulterous escapade with Margo Adams. Deeper investigation showed that Boggs was extremely superstitious and his affair was part of the "good luck" charm syndrome. Other forms of Boggs' superstition revealed a mix of numerology and dietary supplements.

Boggs believed his daily chicken diet aided five .350-plus batting averages in his first seven years in the majors. A cookbook published in 1985 showed his wife in the kitchen with an apron, cooking chicken dishes with such captions as, "When I'm on the road my wife works on new recipes for chicken."

Many baseball fans would be surprised to learn that Boggs was not the first player to espouse an all-chicken diet. Charles Pabor, an outfielder, infielder, pitcher and manager in the pre-National Association days, extolled the virtues of an all-chicken diet in 1871. He was widely known as a strange bird, and sported one of the strangest nicknames in baseball, "The Old Woman in the Red Cap." But he could play. He hit .285 in a pitcher's league, the National Association.

The First Player to Steal and to Slide
Slide, Bobby, Slide!

1865

TOP: The Leatherstocking Base Ball Club of Cooperstown recreated town ball, demonstrating the likely origin of the stolen base in the process. Founder Tom Heitz, attired in top hat and tie, officiates. This form of baseball died out in the 1870s, but was resurrected in Cooperstown during the 1980s.

RIGHT: Ed Cutbert's career spanned the old amateur era and the early professional one. His speed and instincts enabled him to score 453 runs in 452 games, and to become the earliest known player to steal and to slide.

While playing town ball with Tom Heitz, former librarian of the Baseball Hall of Fame, at Cooperstown during the 1980s a startling revelation took place. By following the written rules of 1857, a town ball runner who rounded the stake — base — and turned it loose was forced to go to the next stake. The accidental movement of releasing the base might have caused the idea of stolen bases in the infancy of the sport.

An 1939 documentary about baseball, produced by Lew Fonseca, starred Connie Mack and Clark Griffith. In the film, Bob Addy, an infielder with Rochester in 1869 and five National Association clubs in four years, was introduced as the man who invented sliding in order to gain the first stolen base. The film and the two old stars might be correct. But Henry Chadwick's 1867 system of keeping score had no provision for stolen bases. Edgar Cutbert of the Philadelphia Keystones (amateur) in 1865 performed the first head-first slide to steal a base, which meant that sliding and stealing bases were already happening before Addy played.

Most likely someone who participated in the Fashion Race Course all-star series in 1858, which pitted the best Brooklyn players against the best New Yorkers, was the first to steal a base, but the earliest known now was Ed Cutbert in 1865.

The First Rookie of the Year
Breakthrough for Baseball

1947

TOP: Jackie Robinson and Branch Rickey devised an integration plan that changed the face of baseball and baseball players. In 1947 Robinson was also voted the first Rookie of the Year.

RIGHT: During Jackie Robinson's rookie year he played first base and he led the NL in stolen bases.

Jackie Robinson's major league debut in 1947 was a pivotal event in baseball history, opening the door to racial integration. Enduring intense pressure and racism, Robinson led the NL in stolen bases his rookie year, helping the Dodgers win the pennant.

To take pressure off Jackie Robinson more black players were needed. Three months after Robinson's debut, Larry Doby was signed by Cleveland in the American League. Hank Thompson and Willard Brown soon followed to the Browns. Pitcher Dan Bankhead then joined the Dodgers. Gradually the major league clubs and sportswriters came to accept African-Americans. In fact, the Base Ball Writers Association of America (BBWAA) decided to take their local Chicago-based Rookie of the Year Award national in 1947. With all chapters voting, Jackie Robinson topped an exhilarating year by beating out Larry Jansen of the New York Giants. Separate league selections began two years later. The award then was called the J. Louis Comiskey Memorial Award. Its name was officially changed to the Jackie Robinson Award by Commissioner Peter Ueberroth in the 1987 Hall of Fame induction ceremonies.

The First Fathers and Sons
Junior & Senior

1903

The first son of a major league ballplayer to break into the big leagues was Jack Doescher, who pitched for the Cubs in 1903. His father Herman toiled in numerous major and minor leagues during the nineteenth century. Other more notable father-son combos include Dale and Yogi Berra.

After breaking into the big leagues in 1977, Dale was asked about similarities between himself and his famous father. The young Berra replied, "Our similarities are different." Seldom did sons and sires play the same position. Exceptions were Jim Bagby Senior and Junior and Ed Walsh Senior and Junior; all four pitched. The Sisler family included old man George, who achieved Hall of Fame greatness as a hot hitter with the Browns while also managing them for three years; his son Dick, who hit a late-inning home run to win the 1950 pennant for the Philadelphia Whiz Kids and who also managed; and another son Dave, who pitched for several years. The only other father-son duo to manage was Connie and son Earle Mack. Earle also played for father Connie.

The most famous father-son tandem in recent history was the Griffeys, Ken Senior and Junior, who played together for a real baseball first with the Seattle Mariners in 1990. They even hit home runs in the same game. Other notable father-son duos were the Bonds (Bobby and Barry), Alous (Matty and Moise), Hundleys (Randy and Todd), Stottlemyers (Mel Senior and Mel Junior and Todd), Alomars (Sandy plus Sandy Jr. and Roberto), Ripkens (Cal Senior and Cal Junior and Billy) and many more.

During the 1990s fans saw the first three-generation big league family. Bret Boone made his debut in 1992 as Seattle's second baseman. Bret's father was Bob Boone (1972-90) and his grandfather was Ray Boone (1948-60). Three years later, David Bell, son of Buddy (1972-89) and grandson of Gus (1950-64), made his major league debut for the second three-generation baseball family.

The First Brothers on the Same Team

He Ain't Heavy

BELOW RIGHT: Paul Waner and brother Lloyd — who played together for the Pirates from 1927 to 1940 — instruct their younger sibling in the art of hitting. Lloyd still holds the rookie record with 223 hits and a .355 batting average.

BOTTOM: Paul and Dizzy Dean promised they'd win 50 games in 1934. They won 49 in the regular season (Diz 30 and Paul 19) plus four more (two each) in the World Series.

George and Harry Wright were the sons of Samuel Wright, a cricket professional. Their stellar play in nineteenth century baseball brought a decorum and dignity to the early game of baseball that showed it to be more than a kids' game. They were also the first brothers to be inducted into the Baseball Hall of Fame. The Waners — Lloyd and Paul from Harrah, Oklahoma, who played together in Pittsburgh from 1927 to 1940 — were the second set of Cooperstown-bound brothers.

Generally the youngest of a set of brothers would turn out to be the best. The Bretts, Ken and Bobby, always said "wait until you see baby George." Todd Stottlemyer, the younger, lasted longer and was more effective than brother Mel. Younger brother Roberto has had more success than Sandy Alomar Junior. Stanley Coveleski was a Hall of Fame pitcher and older brother Harry was merely the Giant Killer who ruined the 1908 pennant race for New York fans. The seeming exception was the Dean boys. Although older sibling Dizzy always claimed that the younger Paul was better than him, Dizzy won 150 games while Paul quit with arm problems before his 25th birthday. Ol' Diz bragged that there were more on the farm just like him.

The Dean brag was certainly true for the Boyer brothers, seven of whom played professional baseball, including three — Ken, Cletus and Cloyd — at the major league level. The Alou boys staged a real brother act on September 15, 1963, when all three played in the outfield for one inning for the San Francisco Giants. Felipe, Matty and Jesus were all fine ballplayers but found their greatest impediment to an all-Alou outfield was Willie Mays in center field. As long as brothers continue to play Little League, there will be brothers in the big leagues.

The First Player Banned from Baseball
Outa There!

1866

TOP LEFT: Joe Jackson was banned from baseball for life for his role in the 1919 Black Sox scandal. A great natural hitter, Jackson had batted .356 over 13 years. Babe Ruth patterned his stance and swing after Jackson's.

TOP RIGHT: After being banned for gambling involvement in 1877, Jim Devlin tried many years to be reinstated by baseball but never was.

BOTTOM: Pete Rose appears at the federal court house in Cincinnati in 1990 before being sentenced to prison time for failing to report income.

I n 1865 three players on the New York Mutual Base Ball Club were accused of peculiar fielding that led to 11 runs in the fifth inning of a game versus the Eckfords. William Wansley and Ed Duffy were expelled. Thomas Devyr was ousted and remained under a cloud during the 1866 season, but was reinstated for 1867. Duffy was restored to the lineup by the Mutuals in 1869 because they needed the player. Wansley was finally reinstated in December 1870 by the National Association, but was no longer in demand.

A gambling case that warranted expulsion arose in 1877, when four members of the first place Louisville club were caught red-handed with diamond stickpins and tell-tale telegrams. William Craver, the instigator of the plot, was not banned but was found severely beaten after an International Association contest the following year. Others were George Hall, erstwhile star pitcher James Devlin, and Albert Nichols, all banned from the National League for life. Other leagues accepted the ban and the four Louisville crooks would not play again, nor would they be the last players to be thrown out of baseball.

Pete Rose was the first player banned from the Hall of Fame. Joe Jackson of the 1919 Black Sox had never been declared ineligible — though a prominent Hall of Fame member told the election committee that he would resign if Jackson were elected — until the commissioner wanted to teach Rose a lesson for having embarrassed him in court. Rose and Jackson were banned from the Hall of Fame during the 1990s.

The First Player to Go to War
First in War, First in Peace

1861

Three days after G.I. Hank Greenberg finished serving his military time war was declared, so he re-enlisted. His dramatic return to the big leagues influenced the 1945 pennant race. The first ballplayer to go to war predated Greenberg by eight decades, serving in the Civil War.
OPPOSITE: Ted Williams, Charley Gehringer and Bob Kennedy met at the Jacksonville Naval Air Station for fighter pilot training during World War II.

During World War II, when the military needed manpower, President Franklin Roosevelt was encouraged by baseball super-fan and Postmaster General James A. Farley to issue a statement regarding the national game. Roosevelt wrote, "I honestly feel that it would be best for the country to keep baseball going... These players are a definite recreational asset to their fellow citizens — and that, in my judgment, is worthwhile." Farley and Senator owner Clark Griffith arranged to have the letter published the next day. The commander-in-chief had given baseball a "green light" to play during the war.

America's ballplayers did their part. Whether fighting in distant lands, selling war bonds, or playing ball in the military service, they were there. Ted Williams was a highly decorated fighter pilot. Hoyt Wilhelm and Warren Spahn won Purple Hearts in the Battle of the Bulge, while others, including Billy Southworth, Jr., made the supreme sacrifice. Back home, Brooklyn led all other clubs in selling war bonds. They garnered $180 million in pledges during the 1943 spring drive.

World War I Provost Marshall Enoch Crowder's "Work or Fight" order put baseball on notice that its players were expected to serve their country in useful jobs. Secretary of War Baker dealt baseball a potentially mortal blow when he declared it "non-essential." Throughout every war America's ballplayers have served, in the nineteenth century as well as in the twentieth, and baseball has carried on.

Just as Tiger star Hank Greenberg traded his $50,000 salary for the U.S. Army stipend of $50 a month in 1941, the earliest ballplayers traded their professions for life in the trenches. Civil War veterans with major league experience included Nat Hicks, who served almost five years (1861-65), Oscar Bielaski, Alphonse Martin with the Zouave Regiment, Nick Young, Thomas H. Berry, Harry Berthong, Bill Craver, Chick Fulmer (drummer boy), Scott Hastings, Caleb C. Johnson, Al Pratt and George Zeitlein, who served with Admiral Farragut at New Orleans. Of the group Oscar Bielaski was the oldest, but Nathaniel Hicks had documented service time starting in 1861, so he was likely the first professional ballplayer to serve his country in a military uniform.

Three Playing Streaks

Iron Men

1937
1987
1998

Lou Gehrig shakes hands with Yankee skipper Joe McCarthy as Lou prepared to start his 2,000th consecutive game. His work ethic made him the hero of baseball in the 1930s.

Lou Gehrig was baseball's Iron Man. For 14 years he played every day, never missing a game despite broken bones, beanings, lumbago, severe colds and fatigue. He provided inspiration to a nation caught in the throes of economic depression. More than a symbol, he was a magnificent specimen of manhood and an outstanding player. He captained the Yankees, averaging 153 RBI per season (1927-37). His career 475 home runs included five 40-plus seasons. After 2,130 consecutive games, he took himself out of the lineup in 1937 when his play became hampered by illness. He will always be remembered for his 1939 farewell in Yankee Stadium, where the mortally ill legend announced, "Today, I consider myself the luckiest man on the face of the earth."

Gehrig's consecutive games streak was broken by the son of ballplayer Cal Ripken, Senior. The Orioles' Cal Ripken, Jr. began his streak May 30, 1982. Former opponent Frank White of the Kansas City Royals said that nobody ever hurt Ripken because he was like a block of granite. At 6'4" he was huge for a shortstop. His fielding was worth the price of admission. Although not fast he covered the second base side of the bag as well as his area. In all aspects of the game, he has played and batted with the confidence and skill of a consummate professional. He surpassed Gehrig's streak on September 6, 1995, and ended his own consecutive game streak with 2,632, in 1998.

On the National League side the record was set by one of baseball's flashiest characters, Steve Garvey. Tremendously popular in Los Angeles, Garvey signed with San Diego as a free agent during his record streak of 1,207 games. His streak and playing days came to an end with a broken hand in 1987.

These three streaks became part of baseball lore. The Gehrig streak meant overcoming adversity through sheer hard work. Steve Garvey represented the southern California combination of gutsy performance and style. Amid years of turmoil and change in baseball, Ripken's consistency models commitment and effort, important virtues as the century closes.

Three Player Strikes

Strike Three!

1890
1981
1994

The 1994 strike devastated baseball and left autumn, traditionally reserved for World Series heroics, to early season NFL and college football. At this last game before the strike, fans express their sentiments.

T hree long and grueling strikes have dotted baseball's timeline, in 1890, 1981 and 1994. The first was called the Great Player Rebellion. While the National Brotherhood of Professional Base Ball Players' leaders sailed around the world with the Spalding Tour, the owners passed the Brush Classification Plan, which established categories of salaries for each position. Union leader John M. Ward's remedy would change labor-management relations. Ward started a player-owned league of player-owned teams. The Brotherhood struck the National League and American Association to form the Players' League in 1890. The players won every battle but lost at the peace table when they allowed National League owners to buy into their Players' League franchises.

The second strike could have been called the Lloyd's of London Strike, as the owners settled with the players when their insurance money ran out. Escalating salaries, arbitration and free agency had changed the face of baseball. By 1981 the owners had consistently lost at the bargaining table and in the courts. They wanted player compensation for free-agent losses, and they wanted a victory over the players. The players felt that compensation would limit the number of owners willing to participate in the free-agent draft, so they went on a strike that lasted 50 days.

The last and most serious work stoppage was in 1994, over the salary cap issue. The impasse lasted until March 31, 1995, when the U.S. District Court in Manhattan ordered the owners to reinstate certain provisions of the expired Basic Agreement. The ruling ended an effort by owners to replace the major leaguers with other players, and the season started on April 25, 1995, 255 days after the August 12, 1994 walkout.

The First Player
to Steal 100 in a Season
Brotherhood of Thieves

1962

TOP LEFT: Base thief and future Hall of Famer Rickey Henderson scored 146 runs in 143 games in 1985, the most since Ted Williams' 150 runs in 1949.
TOP RIGHT: The first to steal 100, Maury Wills toiled many years in the minors while waiting for baseball to adopt the running game. When he finally made it to the bigs, Wills emerged as the foremost student of baserunning.
RIGHT: Lou Brock took baserunning lessons from Negro League legend Cool Papa Bell. After a game encounter along the left-field stands, Bell invited Brock to his home to learn the art of stealing third.

*S*tealing is My Game was the title of a book by Maury Wills, the Los Angeles Dodger shortstop who ran the stolen base back into the 1962 record book when he set a new major league single-season record of 104 thefts, shattering Ty Cobb's mark of 96. Using fast legs, a big lead and intense concentration, Wills began a new era in baseball. His intimidating manner caused the rival Giants to leave the sprinkler system on overnight, turning the basepaths into a sea of mud, before a late-season series with the Dodgers. Wills' presence on first base gave a psychological edge to his team. The opposition was prone to make mistakes. The Dodger pressure offense used steals to score runs, not just advance bases. A young Cardinal outfielder named Lou Brock watched Wills and switched from a sometime power hitter to a stolen base threat.

Brock learned Wills' technique of keeping a book on the pitchers' moves to first, the same as batters kept on pitchers' throws to home. The Red Bird led the National League in steals eight of nine seasons during his prime. In the last season of that string, 1974, he stole a record 118 sacks at age 35. Brock passed old-time star Billy Hamilton by one with 938 career steals. Then came the inner city kid with a chip on his shoulder nurtured by a mentor with an even bigger chip.

Rickey Henderson flourished under the tutelage of Oakland manager Billy Martin. Henderson was the ballplayer that Martin wished he could have been. Billy taught Rickey how to crouch at the plate, making the strike zone no bigger than a six-inch square. He explained how to crowd the plate and force the pitcher to serve one up in the wheel-house. Martin gave Henderson the tools and God gave him the talent to become the greatest leadoff batter in baseball history. His first year with the Yankees, Henderson scored more runs than games played. The last player to accomplish that feat was Jimmie Foxx in 1939. Henderson set the single season (130 in 1982) and career stolen base records to go with his other sparkling statistics.

LEAGUES AND TEAMS

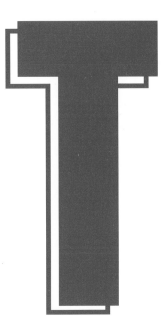

This chapter tells of the formation of teams and leagues, the uniforms the players wore and the equipment they used, as well as the lore of the ballpark. The theme is organization, without which baseball would still be an exercise, or a children's game from whence it came.

Other sports play games that are more event driven and time restricted than baseball. George Will once wrote that football combined the two worst aspects of American society: committee meetings and violence. Perhaps he would include basketball as well, but baseball, on the other hand, combines the American desires for organization and green spaces. The predominant tone of baseball is green, a cool color. America was a beautiful, pastoral country when compared to the cities of Europe from which many nineteenth-century immigrants had come. Americans were looking for a reason to go outside, and baseball gave it to them.

LEFT: Kirby Puckett and Chili Davis celebrate their 1991 World Series victory over the Atlanta Braves after Game Seven's extra-inning heroics.
BELOW: The Chicago White Stockings of the 1880s were known as the team of six-footers and for their infield "Stonewall Defense."

Another reason for baseball's success is that it is a young man's game, run by older and wiser former players. Albert Spalding and Albert Reach represented the ultimate success of a player. The central story of many children's books in the first two decades of this century adapted the rags to riches Horatio Alger story to baseball. Baseball Joe and Lefty Locke were both fiction characters who spanned the gamut from high school busher to club owner and league president. Joe Cronin was a twentieth-century Baseball Joe just as Spalding was the nineteenth-century Lefty Locke, ascending from pitcher to magnate and saviour of baseball. Writers and dreamers and players were able to picture themselves climbing the "corporate ladder" of baseball because the structure existed. Sometimes the structure became unbalanced, as in Robert Coover's cult baseball novel, *Universal Baseball Association Incorporated, J. Henry Waugh,* or in the 1890 Player Rebellion, but the National Pastime always solved its problems with baseball solutions. Sometimes there were crazy solutions, as the uniforms color-coded by position (1882) that you will read about. And other times the solutions were years too soon, as with numbers on uniforms.

The reason why baseball survives is its adaptability. When the game fails to adapt we fans will be watching the demise of the National Pastime, and this book will be a historical document, but for now it is informative and, hopefully, enjoyable reading.

GEO. F. GORE.   FRANK S. FLINT   A. C. ANSON, JAS. H. McCORMICK,   M. J. KELLY.   FRED H. PFEFFER.
CENTER FIELD.   CATCHER.   CAPTAIN AND 1ST BASE.   PITCHER.   RIGHT FIELD AND CATCHER.   2D BASE.
EDWARD N. WILLIAMSON.   A. DALRYMPLE.   THOS. E. BURNS.   JOHN G. CLARKSON,   W. A. SUNDAY.
3D BASE.   LEFT FIELD.   SHORT STOP.   PITCHER.   RIGHT FIELD.
CHICAGO BASE BALL CLUB.

Leagues

The First Professional League
A Real Players' League

1871

The National Association of Professional Base Ball Players (NA) was the first professional league. It was formed in the spring of 1871 when the amateurs withdrew from the National Association of Base Ball Players. For several years the debate had raged about the use of paid players. The fully professional Cincinnati Red Stockings were considered an expensive novelty. When they finally lost and disbanded in 1870, the amateurs decided to act. By withdrawing to form their own organization they left the NA to the pros.

In the organizational meeting on March 17 at Colliers on Broadway in New York, delegates from the leading professional clubs voted to accept the same rules and regulations as they previously had used under the amateur banner. Representatives from 10 teams showed up, but only eight teams took the field that first year. They were the Athletics (Philadelphia), Haymakers (Troy, New York), Olympics (Washington), Red Stockings (Boston), Forest City (Rockford), Forest City (Cleveland), White Stockings (Chicago), Mutuals (New York), and the Kekiongas (Fort Wayne, Indiana). The first officers were president James W. Kerns, vice president J. F. Evans, secretary Nick Young, and treasurer J. W. Schofield. Teams could compete for the pennant by paying $10. The banner would go to the club winning the highest number of series, which was the best of five games and had to be arranged individually by each nine. In practice, the eastern teams went on western road trips to Ft. Wayne, Chicago, Rockford and Cleveland, and vice versa. Although the National Association marked the beginnings of major league baseball, the player-controlled league was rife with organizational and financial problems, and lasted for only five seasons.

The First Owners' League
Hulbert's Enterprise

1876

William Hulbert was a champion of Chicago. He retorted, "I'd rather be a lamp post in Chicago than a millionaire in any other city." He brought the National League to the Windy City in 1876.

The National League of Professional Base Ball Clubs effectively replaced the National Association of Professional Base Ball Players at its founding on February 2, 1876, at the Grand Central Hotel in New York City. The old NA league had been unable or unwilling to prohibit gambling or to control contract jumping — called "revolving." Chicago White Stockings president William Hulbert, who organized the meeting of the leading East Coast teams, presented a constitution which declared the objectives of the new league: First — To encourage, foster and elevate the game of Base Ball; Second — To enact and enforce proper rules for the exhibition and conduct of the game; Third — To make Base Ball playing respectable and honorable. The document was embraced by all, and Morgan Bulkeley of Hartford was elected president of the new league.

Known today as the National League, Hulbert's enterprise was a grand success. Fighting off challengers in the nineteenth century, signing a peace treaty with the upstart American League in 1903, flourishing during the integration of the 1940s, and expanding in the post-World War II era, the National League has survived with one original team still intact: the Chicago Cubs.

The First Minor League
An International League

1877

The International
Association champs, from
London, Ontario, were
the Tecumsehs.

L. C. Waite, the secretary of the St. Louis Red Stockings, sent out circulars calling for non-league clubs to band together, charge their own prices and operate independently of the National League. The idea resulted in a convention at Pittsburgh on February 20, 1877. Pitcher Candy Cummings, of the Live Oaks of Lynn, was named president of the International Association of Professional Base Ball Players (IA) by delegates representing 17 clubs. Other officers were H. Gorman as vice president and James Williams as secretary.

Set up as a sort of rival of the National League rather than as a minor league, the organization soon became subordinate. The old mistakes of the National Association were repeated in that no regular schedule was adopted, any club paying the fee could compete for the championship, and there were no territorial restrictions or protection. A club could join without competing for the pennant and become a sort of association member. A 25-cent admission to the games was charged. Despite its defects many players preferred to play in the International Association rather than the National League.

The better International clubs were as good, or better, than second division League teams. The competitive IA teams during the league's brief existence were the London Tecumsehs (Ontario), Pittsburgh Alleghenies, Columbus Buckeyes, Lynn Live Oaks, Guelph Maple Leafs, plus the Rochester and Manchester Base Ball Clubs. The champions of Canada and of the Association were the London Tecumsehs. Unfortunately, the International Association lasted only two years.

The First Rival Major League
Sunday Ball and Free-flowing Beer

1882

When four players of the 1876–77 Louisville team were suspended for throwing games, Louisville quit the NL. Backers of the club began to push for a new league. The first American Association featured Louisville, St. Louis, Cincinnati and Philadelphia, all teams blackballed by the NL.

The founding of the American Association in 1882 gave the National League a viable opponent for post-season play, but the two leagues did not look favorably at the situation. The Association was raucous, rambunctious and ambitious. It was formed by players, club owners and saloon keepers who were disgruntled by the "high-handed actions" by National League president William Hulbert. Since 1876, Philadelphia, New York, St. Louis, Louisville and Cincinnati had been expelled or forced from the league.

Cincinnati was particularly incensed by their treatment of being expelled for not agreeing to prohibit the sale of beer and Sunday games. The sporting society of St. Louis and Cincinnati hosted meetings in Pittsburgh and Cincinnati where Denny McKnight, active in the old International Association, was elected president of the American Association of Professional Base Ball Clubs. The teams of the new league — Philadelphia, St. Louis, Cincinnati, Louisville, Pittsburgh and Baltimore — featured 25-cent admission, free-flowing beer and Sunday games. The new league enjoyed a heyday, but lasted only until 1891, when disputes with the National League over the spoils of the newly defunct Players' League led to its demise.

J. C. Carbine - W. L. Hague - W. S. Hastings - Chas. Fulmer - A. Devlin - J. C. Chapman Snyder - J. J. Gerhardt - A. A. Auison -

G. W. Bechtel - J. J. Ryan.

1876.

The First Reserve Clause
The Game's Foundation

1879

Dave McNally (pictured) and Andy Messersmith changed the philosophy and economy of baseball by their successful challenge of the reserve system.

Dodgers right-hander Andy Messersmith and veteran Dave McNally "played out their options" in 1975 by refusing to sign contracts. After the season, arbitrator Peter Seitz ruled that players who did not sign their contracts could not be held to the Reserve Clause for more than its one-year option provision. Dave McNally and Andy Messersmith were declared free agents. The owners challenged the ruling in Kansas City Federal Court. The effort to void the declaration failed. The old reserve system, which dated from September 29, 1879, was dead.

The old reserve system, established to prevent players from signing two or more contracts, then choosing which one they'd honor, served baseball well and gave the fans and owners consistency. Today baseball has struggled and has yet to prove it can thrive without the consistency that the Reserve Clause gave to the national game.

The First League of all African-American Players

We are the Ship: Rube's League

1920

TOP: The Chicago American Giants were charter members of the Negro National League formed by Rube Foster in 1920.
BOTTOM: The Kansas City Monarchs of 1936 became so successful as a barnstorming team that they led the effort to reform the Negro League.

The Negro National League was founded in Kansas City, Missouri, on February 13, 1920, by a group of black independent club owners called together by Andrew "Rube" Foster. The group wanted a vehicle for lowering the percentage of gate receipts taken by eastern booking agents. By forming the National Association of Professional Colored Base Ball Leagues, then the Negro National League, they found strength in an association through which they could sign contracts and book games in major league stadiums.

The members of the original Negro National League were the Chicago American Giants, Chicago Giants, St. Louis Giants, Detroit Stars, Taylor ABCs, Cuban Stars, and the Kansas City Monarchs. The league's early stars were Oscar Charleston, John Henry Lloyd, Joe Williams, Bullet Rogan and Cristobal Torriente. Within three years, the league and its players were drawing 400,000 paying customers, and achieved the stability that Foster had sought for black baseball.

The organized black league created one of the largest African-American-owned businesses in North America. In 1923 the white East Coast booking agents, who had been accustomed to taking 50 percent of the gate for expenses, started the East Colored League to compete with the Negro National. The natural rivalry led to five hotly contested Colored World Series from 1924 through 1928.

The successful planning and implementation of Foster's Negro National League had far-reaching impacts on more than the National Pastime. The league and its success came at a time when African-Americans were forging their own national character and style. The league's heyday was also the heyday of the American city and its culture.

The First Professional Women's League
A League of their Own

1943

The All-American Girls Professional Baseball League (AAGPBL) was almost forgotten until the Public Broadcasting System produced a special that spawned the movie, *A League of their Own*. Directed by Penny Marshall and starring Geena Davis, Lori Petty, Rosie O'Donnell, Tom Hanks and Madonna, it sparked public interest in the women's league of the 1940s. The real league was even more exciting than the movie.

Four teams — Rockford Peaches, South Bend Blue Sox, Racine Belles, and Kenosha Comets — opened the 1943 season. In the initial year, the league, a brainstorm of Philip K. Wrigley, who wanted to fill his ballpark during the wartime manpower shortage, drew 176,000 fans. At its peak, the AAGPBL was seen by more than a million paying customers in 1948. Two years later, the league would fire its $50,000 per year publicity man, Arthur Meyeroff, a move that caused the league to go rapidly downhill. The league's directors never intended for it to survive the war, but it did survive because the attraction was to skilled women baseball players, not females trying to play baseball. Former president Gerald Ford watched his hometown Grand Rapids Chicks battle basestealing phenom Sophie Kuries, who had 202 steals in 204 attempts, and Dorothy Kamenshek, the woman Connie Mack claimed he would pay $100,000 for if she were allowed to play in the majors.

The establishment and success of the All-American Girls Professional Baseball League gave young girls heroines in the world of sports.

The First Little League Teams
Fielding Dreams

RIGHT: The Northridge, California, team celebrates a victory over Springfield, Virginia, in the 1994 World Series, carrying on the spirit set in motion by the first Little League teams in 1938.

BELOW: Members of the Guadalupe, Mexico, team take a victory lap after defeating the USA team 5–4 in a thrilling-come-from-behind win to gain the 1997 Little League World Championship.

I n 1988 Carl Stotz received a letter from President Ronald Reagan commending him for starting the Little League baseball program in 1938. Stotz had wanted a place for his two nephews to play competitive baseball under consistent rules while wearing standard uniforms. His museum, in his Williamsport (Pennsylvania) home, detailed the beginnings of the league. It was later transferred to the Little League headquarters in another section of Williamsport.

Little League wasn't the only youth baseball program. The American Legion baseball program was founded in 1925. Baseball and boys went together until the 1970s, when girls were admitted to most amateur programs. Now the circle of baseball was complete. It encompassed all races and both sexes, yet remained the same competitive game as envisioned in 1845 when the Knickerbockers drew up the rules. Another fact has also remained true through the ages. Tomorrow's fans were yesterday's ballplayers.

Many organizations have supported youth leagues. The Little League, YMCA, RBI (Revitalizing Baseball in the Inner city), Pony, Colt, Khouri, Babe Ruth, 3&2, Boys & Girls Clubs, and Police Athletic League have featured leagues for kids. When the youngsters grew up, they could play in the American Legion, Stan Musial, Ban Johnson, Sandy Koufax, or Connie Mack leagues. For the college-aged youth, eight NCAA-affiliated summer leagues existed. The real winners are the kids who have so many opportunities to play.

Clubs

Dick McBride

The First Team to Win the National Association Pennant
The First League Champs

1871

TOP LEFT: The Athletics, the oldest continuous nickname in baseball, won the first professional pennant, but were forced out of the league for failing to make the last road trip in 1876. The club members turned their interests to cricket, where they won the world title in 1878.

TOP RIGHT: A's winning pitcher Dick McBride.

The Great Chicago Fire of 1871 raged three days and completely burned up the White Stockings' ballpark, club house and players' belongings. It threatened to destroy the first pennant race as the White Stockings had several more scheduled games versus the Philadelphia Athletics and Troy Haymakers. To make matters worse, when the Chicago club went east to play their rescheduled games, bad weather pre-empted most of the championship games. The championship committee, controlled by the Athletics, decreed that the winner of a contest at the Brooklyn ballpark between Chicago and Philadelphia would be the league champ.

Chicago appeared in all hues of uniforms while the Philly bunch came ready to play. Only some loose play in the last inning averted a shutout by Athletic pitcher Dick McBride as Philadelphia won, 4-1. The whip pennant flew over Philadelphia's ballpark at 15th and Columbia. The winning team had played together at the Athletic Base Ball Club for many years, and some played cricket as well. McBride, John Radcliffe, Wes Fisler, Al Reach and Count Sensenderfer were veteran stars. Recent additions Levi Meyerle, Fergy Malone and Ed Cutbert rounded out the starting nine.

CINCINNATIS.
CHAMPIONS 1882.

The First Teams in Post-Season Play
A Nineteenth-Century World Series

1882

Cincinnati, winners of the initial American Association flag in 1882, scheduled post-season games with Chicago, holders of the National League banner. Two games were played when Association president Denny McKnight stepped in and threatened to expel Cincy if they continued to defy the ban on playing NL teams. Cincinnati had taken Chicago 4-0 on a seven-hit shutout by Will White. The second tiff was another whitewash. This time Chicago's Larry Corcoran bested Will White 2-0 on three hits. No more games were played. The real World Series would start two years later.

Post-season championship play began in 1884 when the New York Mets (Association) arranged a series to be played in Gotham City against the powerful League champion Providence Grays. Although betting on games was usually rampant, little wagering took place because the Grays' pitcher, Old Hoss Radbourn, had won 60 games that year. He proved too much for the Mets as he disposed of them in three straight games, and the tradition of post-season play had begun.

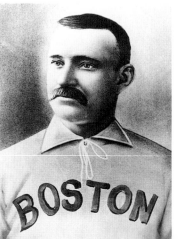

The First Team to Win the National League Pennant
Are These Really the Cubs?

BELOW: The 1876 Chicago White Stockings, winners of the first NL pennant, featured two future Hall of Fame players, Al Spalding and Cap Anson. However, the star of the season was Roscoe Barnes (RIGHT), who led the NL in batting, runs, hits, total bases, on-base percentage and slugging average.

1876

The Chicago White Stockings (later called the Cubs), led by League founders William Hulbert, Albert Spalding and Cap Anson, would have been extremely embarrassed if they had not won the first National League pennant in 1876. After all, they had engineered the downfall of the old Association by signing its best players and withdrawing from the group.

The real star of the first NL flag bearers was Ross Barnes, an accomplished fair-foul hitter. The stroke, in which a batter intentionally strikes the ball downward with spin to cause it to land in fair territory but shoot foul a few feet in front of the plate, was banned the following winter and Barnes, who sus-

tained an injury and lost his favorite batting stroke, was never the same ballplayer. But in 1876 he torched the league, leading in runs, hits, doubles, triples, walks, batting, slugging, and on-base and fielding averages. He scored 126 runs in only 66 games. The team was so set in its lineup that it had only two substitutes all season.

SCENES AT THE CENTENNIAL EXHIBITION GROUNDS.

ANSON GLENN A.G. SPALDING BARNES BIELASKI

ADDY PETERS

ANDRUS JAS. WHITE McVEY HINES

THE WHITE STOCKING BASE BALL CLUB OF CHICAGO, AS ORGANIZED FOR THE SEASON OF 1876.

The First Team to Win the American League Pennant

Are These Really the White Sox?

1901

The Chicago White Stockings won the first AL pennant. Ban Johnson guided the fledging American League through start-up turmoil. He established the principle that baseball is good family entertainment.

Cincinnati sportswriter Ban Johnson's reformed Western League was renamed the American League in 1900. The intention was to challenge the National League in 1901. As league president, Johnson still had a few bugs to work out.

His new league respected umpires at a time when its rival, the National League, set new lows in abusive behavior toward its fans, officials and players. The first season produced a wild pennant race. A problem occurred when other clubs felt that the AL's Chicago White Stockings, owned by Charles Comiskey, had won because they systematically intimidated the umpires, and that Ban Johnson, who quashed rowdy behavior by Detroit, had done nothing, and maybe even rooted for the Chicago club.

The next season the other AL teams decided to bully the umpires, but when the White Stockings attempted it they were severely punished. Finally a spitting incident led to a powwow between Johnson, John McGraw, Joe McGinnity, umpire Tommy Connally and Charles Comiskey (all Hall of Famers), who met to mete out justice. One player, McGinnity, was reinstated; another, Jack Katoll, was banned for life; and umpires were given league approval to rule each contest. After the September 1901 meeting the American League seldom suffered from the violence that sometimes characterized the National League.

The '02 flag flew above the Athletics' park at 29th and Columbia, 14 blocks from the site of Philly's first professional flag. The Athletics, led by Connie Mack, featured three 30-plus game winners, including future Hall of Famers Eddie Plank and Rube Waddell.

The First Team to Win
100 Major League Games
The City on the Hill

1892

TOP LEFT: Star Boston pitcher Kid Nichols was key to Boston's record 1892 season, tossing 35 of their 102 wins.

TOP RIGHT: Ace pitcher Jack Stivetts, originally a Brownie, joined Boston when the old AA folded after the 1891 season.

RIGHT: Recent Hall of Fame inductee Frank Selee built two dynasties, the 1890s Beaneaters and the 1900s Cubs.

The best team of the 1890s was neither the slugging Spiders nor the brawling Orioles, but the scientific Boston Beaneaters. Led by near-genius Frank Selee, the Beaneaters won five pennants during the decade. They set a nineteenth-century record with 102 wins in 1892 and then again in 1898. Selee, who later built the Chicago Cubs' dynasty, molded an air-tight infield with a resourceful outfield and a youthful pitching staff. They met and defeated the Spiders and Orioles in head-to-head competition. The Beaneaters' infield of Jimmy Collins, Herman Long, Bobby Lowe and Fred Tenney could hit as well as they could field. The talented outfield was even better.

Hugh Duffy and Tommy McCarthy, called the Heavenly Twins by Boston fans, performed difficult hit-and-run plays. Their "scientific baseball" presented a stark contrast to the habits of the Orioles and Spiders. Neither of the Beaneaters' arch foes could field pitchers to match Kid Nichols, with 300 victories by age 31, and Jack Stivetts, who won 35 games while batting .296 in 1892 and went 11-4 with a .367 average in 1897, both pennant-winning years for Boston.

The First Team to Employ Scouts
Scaring up the Game

1868

Aaron Champion (**BELOW RIGHT**) took advantage of a new idea when he appointed businessman George Ellard (**BELOW LEFT**) to secure the services of baseball's brightest and best for the 1869 Cincinnati Red Stockings team (**LEFT**).

George B. Ellard and Alfred T. Goshorn were appointed as a committee by Aaron Champion, president of the Cincinnati Red Stockings, to make arrangements with Harry Wright and his brother George to secure their services for the 1869 year. Ellard at that time owned the largest sporting goods establishment in the West. His many acquaintances throughout the baseball world enabled him to choose from the best players for the new Cincinnati nine. With the help of Harry Wright, who had been captain of the 1868 Cincinnati team, George Ellard selected the baseball team that made Cincinnati famous.

The success of the 1868-69 Cincinnati Red Stockings proved that planning and scouting can reap huge dividends. Other clubs sought to utilize scouting. Until paid scouts came along, scouting systems were really a system of friendship. Such managers as John McGraw or Connie Mack possessed huge networks of baseball acquaintances, including coaches and former players. This network gave them first choice on talented youngsters. Sometimes the system broke down, as it seemed to in the case of Babe Ruth.

Both McGraw and Mack went to their graves believing that they had been cheated out of Babe Ruth by Jack Dunn, owner of the Baltimore Orioles. Both claimed that they had the right of first refusal. However, all was fair in love and scouting.

The First Team to Go from Last to First
The Last Shall be First

1890

There was much written and spoken about the sensational turnabout of the Atlanta Braves and Minnesota Twins in 1991 when they met in the World Series. The previous year both had finished in last place. The achievement was put into context when historians brought to life the sad but true case of the "Worst to First to next to Worst" Louisville Colonels.

The 1889 American Association Louisville Colonels finished dead last, 27 ½ games behind the seventh place Kansas City Cowboys. The next year, with seven regulars — including two pitchers — from that dreadful squad, the Louisville nine won the flag by 10 games on the strength of an 88-44 record, an improvement of 64 wins. The next season when the stars came back from the Players' League, Louisville went back to their customary location at the bottom, where they barely beat out Washington for seventh place. The squad started the 1891 season with the same team that had won the pennant the year before.

The First Farm Club
Recipe for Success

1920

Branch Rickey had an idea for competing with the rich clubs who constantly outbid him for young prospects. He wanted to place youngsters with minor league clubs, teaching and seasoning them until they were ready for the majors. What he needed was a chain of clubs that the Cardinals owned outright or had operating agreements to test his idea. St. Louis owner Sam Breadon endorsed the idea. The first club in the Cardinals' farm system was Houston (Texas League) who joined in 1920, then Ft. Smith in the Western Association. At the 1921 annual National Association meeting, Rickey purchased half interest in the Syracuse club from its ine-briated owner for $50,000. The Cardinals' miniscule farm system grew into an empire. Other clubs noticed the farm advantage.

The wealthy Yankees, the kind of club that Breadon and Rickey hoped to defeat, embraced the farm concept. General Manager Ed Barrow built a Cadillac version of the farm system. In 1938 the top Yankee farm teams, Newark and Kansas City, confronted each other in the Junior World Series. Control over players brought the farm systems into conflict with Commiss-ioner Landis. In sweeping sanctions the irascible judge emanci-pated 91 of the Cardinal serfs, then 18 months later, he freed a similar number of baby Tigers from the Detroit system. Regardless of how Landis looked upon the farm system, it was credited with providing a steady source of players while building major league fans in minor league towns.

Bush   McInnis   Barry   Collins   Baker   Mgr. Mack   Oldring   Thomas

Middle Row: Daley, Schang, Lapp, Brown, Bender, Wyckoff, Davis, Orr. *Bottom Row:* Houck, E. Murphy, Plank, Strunk, Bailey, D. Murphy, Walsh, Taff

The First Championship Club to be Broken up
Fire Sale!

1915

TOP: After winning three World Championships in five years, A's manager Connie Mack sold off his stars. By 1916, only McInnis, Walsh, Schang, Strunk, Oldring and Bush were left from the 1913 World Champion Athletics, pictured above.

BELOW RIGHT: Marlins owner Wayne Huizenga proved that cash and brains coupled with good management can win a World Series title. But after 1997 he dismantled the championship team.

During the nineteenth century both participants in the 1886 World Championships —Chicago White Stockings and St. Louis Browns — sold star players to their rivals, but developed more talent to continue their winning ways. Later others would disassemble championship clubs, allowing fans to suffer.

After winning four pennants and three World Championships in five years, Philadelphia A's manager Connie Mack sold Eddie Collins to the White Sox for $50,000 in order to keep him in the American League instead of losing him to the Federal League, where A's pitchers Eddie Plank and Chief Bender had fled. Bob Shawkey, Herb Pennock, Eddie Murphy and Jack Barry were traded during the 1915 season. Frank "Home Run" Baker sat out the year in protest of Mack's dealings. The A's finished in last place for seven straight years.

Cash-poor Mack rebuilt the A's in the late 1920s, won three pennants, then sold his stars again. Al Simmons, Jimmy Dykes and Mule Haas went to the White Sox for $100,000 in 1933. The next year, Tom Yawkey, owner of the Red Sox, kept Mack's operation afloat by purchasing Lefty Grove, Rube Walberg and Max Bishop for a cool $125,000.

Five decades later it took Marlins owner Wayne Huizenga five years to build World Champions in Florida, and five months to tear them down. Gone from 1997 were position players Moises Alou, Bobby Bonilla, Charles Johnson, Gary Sheffield, Devon White and Jeff Conine. Trades of pitchers Wilson Alvarez, Robb Nen, Kevin Brown and Al Leiter brought the Marlins dozens of top prospects. The "Fighting Fish" may have the last laugh as they acquired players who can make them competitive for the next 10 years.

The First Teams to Play a Doubleheader

Let's Play Two!

1882

The 1882 Providence Grays, who played a doubleheader with Worcester in 1882, featured stars. Front row **(LEFT TO RIGHT)** are Charlie Reilly, Sandy Nava, Barney Gilligan; middle row are Tom York, Joe Start, Harry Wright, George Wright, Monte Ward; top row are Paul Hines, Jerry Denny, Hoss Radbourn, Jack Farrell. The two Wrights, Ward and Radbourn are all in the Hall of Fame.

Doubleheader was a railroad term, meaning two engines back-to-back. Two games on one day had been fairly common since 1873, especially on Decoration (May 31) and Independence (July 4) Days when rivals played home-and-home, morning and afternoon games. The first two-game day occurred on July 4, 1873, when the Elizabeth Resolutes split with the Boston Red Stockings, winning 11-2 and losing 32-3.

On September 25, 1882, the Worcester Brown Stockings started a baseball tradition by hosting Providence for two games while charging only one admission. The Worcester and Troy teams had already been informed that their membership in the National League would not be renewed. The two clubs played their two remaining games with each other, drawing 6, in the rain, and 25 paying fans for the two contests. Not even a doubleheader could save them.

At the Ballpark

The First Ballpark to Burn
Mrs. O'Leary's Cow

1871

A general view after the Chicago fire reveals the devastation that ended the White Stockings' run for the 1871 National Association pennant.

Fire has always been the greatest threat to civilization. The Assyrians shot flaming arrows into walled fortresses to intimidate opponents. The Syrians used burning pitch to discourage attacking soldiers. Byzantine sailors shot flaming tar — Greek Fire — that ignited when it hit water, and it stuck to the sides of ships. America's smartest man, Ben Franklin, started a fire engine company and an insurance company. Fire destroyed ballparks.

In Chicago on October 8, 1871, a small blaze, whipped by high winds, became a towering inferno. For three days the fire raged. The first area to go was near the docks where the ballpark was located. Within the first 24 hours the White Stockings lost their clubhouse, their uniforms, all their equipment and the ballpark. Games which had a bearing on the National Association pennant race had to be replayed back East where bad weather and storms were also cancelling games. The league decided to play one game for the championship. Chicago lost and finished third.

Fires forced club owners to build better, bigger and safer ballparks. In their search to build a better ballpark, they found the most modern technology and had to borrow money to finance the construction. The act of borrowing money forced club owners to construct business plans that included long range financial projections. This made baseball a more sound and efficient business.

The First Ballpark to be Enclosed and to Charge Admission
Union Grounds

1862

Enclosed ballparks enabled teams to charge admission, which paid for professionalism. Here is Opening Day, May 4, 1869, in Cincinnati. The "Reds" won 88 straight games over a two-year period.

Enclosed parks and admission signalled the beginning of the end of baseball as an amateur sport. When William H. Cammeyer opened his new park on May 15, 1862, paying customers (15-cent entry fee) made it possible for prominent New York and Brooklyn clubs to play for a share of the "gate money." When the grounds opened, a band was on hand to celebrate the event. It patriotically played "The Star Spangled Banner," the first time music accompanied a ball game.

The earliest enclosed park, Cammeyer's Union Grounds in Brooklyn, was primitive compared with our modern stadiums, or even the ballparks of a couple of decades later, but in those days it was considered an attraction to Brooklynites. The grandstand was a long wooden shed, supplied with benches for the ladies. Additional benches interspersed about the grounds made it possible to seat about 1500 people. Others watched from the sidelines, and on days of big crowds police were on hand to keep order. In one corner of the field there was a clubhouse large enough for three teams. There were also several other buildings, one a saloon, the others probably used for collection of admissions and storing equipment. A fence six or seven feet high enclosed the entire grounds. The area covered at least six acres. Outfielders pulled down balls that could fly as far as 500 feet without hitting a fence.

The First Ballpark with an Exploding Scoreboard
Chicago Crowd Pleaser

1959

Bill Veeck purchased the Chicago White Sox from Charles Comiskey and his sister Dorothy Rigney in 1959 after prolonged negotiations. He promised South Side fans a cracking good time, and he delivered.

The club won the American League pennant in Veeck's first year of ownership. He followed the exciting year with the unveiling of his *piece de resistance*, the exploding scoreboard. He got the idea from watching a pinball machine. He wanted to adapt the exploding, light-flashing, flag-waving graphics of winning a jackpot to baseball.

Veeck built the Comiskey scoreboard with 10 mortars bristling from the top for firing Roman candles. The fireworks crew, behind the scoreboard, exploded off bombs, rockets and firecrackers. They shot off fireworks for every home run that the White Sox hit. Veeck claimed that exploding scoreboard was the best idea he ever had. Cleveland was offered the idea before he purchased the White Sox, but refused it, for the better in Chicago.

The First Ladies Day
Ladies First

1887

Former player, manager and owner Abner Powell experimented with promotions geared to entertain the crowd. Rain checks and ladies days were two of his better ideas.

Abner Powell, ballplayer and entrepreneur, received credit for starting Ladies Day on April 29, 1887, in New Orleans of the Southern League. While accounts gave no indication that ladies were granted discount tickets, they were received as special guests as they "came in carriages, buggies, in their spring attire, and made the cozy grandstand a bower of beauty."

Actually both Cincinnati in 1876 and Syracuse in 1877 allowed women to attend games free or at reduced rates because their appearance kept down rowdiness in the grandstand. The paper reported that a handful of grumbling men were forced to leave the grandstand to go to the rail to smoke and carry on. The image-conscious Syracuse crowd would later suggest that screens and gates be used to keep the lower classes from mixing with those in the grandstand.

The 1909 St. Louis Browns institutionalized Ladies Days. Robert Hedges, owner, prohibited the sale of alcoholic beverages on these special occasions, and always kept a handful of tickets to give to anyone accompanying a wife, mother, sweetheart or daughter.

The First Seventh-Inning Stretch
Sing It, Harry!

1870s

Carrying on the tradition originating in the 1870s, the late Cubs announcer Harry Caray used the "seventh-inning stretch" to exercise his vocal cords and reaffirm the crowd's allegiance to baseball. He was wildly popular late in his life.

When President William H. Taft got up to leave the opening game of the 1910 season in Washington, his entourage followed. Fans, seeing a large mass of people standing, also stood. It was the seventh inning and a legend had been born about the origin of the seventh-inning stretch. In reality, fans had been standing and stretching at about the seventh inning since the early 1870s when Boston fans, aware that their team scored a large number of runs in the seventh inning, became accustomed to rising and cheering on the hometown boys.

During the baseball season of 1887, Father Jasper, in charge of physical education of the Manhattan College faculty, used the gathering at ball games to promote his physical fitness regime. Students rose in the Manhattan half of the seventh to perform calisthenics.

Years later the late Harry Caray personally led Chicago Cubs fans in the singing of "Take Me Out to the Ball Game," at Wrigley Field. When he died, his wife Duchie made frequent Wrigley appearances, where Harry's grandson Skip Caray took his grandsire's place at the microphone.

The First Concrete and Reinforced Steel Ballpark

If You Build it, They will Come

1909

The Pirates celebrated
the premiere of Forbes
Field with a World Series
title in 1909. Notice the
left field fence where, 51
years later, the Yankees'
Yogi Berra would watch
Bill Mazeroski's home
run sail over his head to
win the 1960 World Series
in the bottom of the ninth,
ushering in a new era.

The building of stadiums precipitated the era of big business. No longer did a club operate on a proverbial shoestring. The building of the ballparks required financing, and sometimes deficit borrowing, and produced an asset that tied clubs to their cities and fans. The legions who tramped to the ballpark also required plans for crowd control, such as traffic flow for entering and exiting. These beloved playing-field monuments lasted 65 to 70 years and became symbols of baseball lore and the objects of nostalgia.

The Giants' record attendance of 910,000 in 1908 astonished the other club owners. They immediately wanted to increase the seating capacities at their ballparks. This desire and technological advances in steel and reinforced concrete construction led to an era of ballpark building. In 1909, Shibe Park in Philadelphia paved the way as new and spacious cathedrals such as Sportsman's Park in St. Louis, and Forbes Field in Pittsburgh, opened their turnstiles to the public . The following year, League Park in Cleveland and Comiskey Park in Chicago were in use. In 1911 the spacious Griffith Stadium greeted fans, followed by Fenway Park and Navin Field in 1912, Ebbets Field in 1913, Weeghman Park (now called Wrigley Field) in 1914, and finally Braves Field — with 56,000 squeezed into 40,000 seats on Opening Day — in 1915.

In futuristic contrast, tall as a 31-story building, Toronto's SkyDome opened on June 5, 1989, and a new phenomenon started. Every game sold out for the rest of the year. Then, every game in 1990 sold out. Cities readily invested in new and expensive ballparks in Baltimore, Arlington, Cleveland, Denver and Atlanta. Their games sold out. The third era of ballpark building had begun in earnest.

The First "Knot-Hole" Section

Sponsoring Little Rascals

1918

When the Cardinals developed
the knot-hole idea, treating
young fans to free games, the
public service quickly caught on.

The knot-hole section idea laid the foundation for the St. Louis Cardinals' dynasty to cross generations and cover more than 15 states. Sam Breadon started the ball rolling when he owned but four shares of Cardinal stock in 1918. At the suggestion of insurance agent W. E. Bilheimer, a bleacher ticket was given to a needy boy for every share of stock. The later program offered a free seat as a weekday bonus to boys and girls. The idea filtered down to the minor leagues.

Tulsa and other dozens of Cardinals affiliates ran knot-hole clubs. Sometimes, as in Tulsa, the boys and girls actually sat outside the stadium on a special row of seats attached to the fence. The youngsters watched the action through wire mesh that covered a two-foot high slit in the fence, the modern version of a knot-hole.

The First Hot Dogs at Ball Games

Get them While they're Hot!

1880s

Hot dogs and baseball go together. Here sons of Robert Vogeler, an American businessman who spent over a year in a Hungarian jail on espionage charges, enjoy both, watching a Giants–Cubs game at the Polo Grounds in 1951, as personal guests of Manager Leo Durocher.

Humphrey Bogart made a commercial about baseball; he said, "A hot dog at the game beats roast beef at the Ritz." The hot dog served a marvelous purpose. It was cheap and salty, which encouraged the eater to buy drinks. It also put something into the stomach of a fellow who might have had too many beers. Unfortunately, the standard hot dog has become passe. More expensive and more nutritional foods have replaced the dog and beer.

The origin of the hot dog has been in dispute. Cartoonist Tad Dorgan drew the hot dog at the St. Louis World's Fair in 1904, and America learned of a new food. But was it really new?

Germans in Cincinnati, Louisville, Milwaukee and St. Louis had been putting sausage in bread wraps for eating at ball games since the 1880s. The patrons there washed down their dogs with free-flowing beer. The first hot dogs eaten by fans were likely consumed at American Association games during the 1880s.

Ring Lardner wrote a sketch for the Ziegfield Follies in which a relief pitcher was munching a hot dog on the bullpen bench when he was suddenly summoned to the mound. "Who's up?" he asked the bullpen catcher. "Cobb, Crawford and Veach," was the reply. "Here hold this puppy," the pitcher said, "I'll be right back."

The First Use of a Tarpaulin
Rain Delay!

1888

Adapted to baseball in 1888, the tarp idea was quickly adopted by the NL. The unrolling of the tarp became a familiar sight on rainy days, as pictured here at Ebbets Field in 1952, when everyone had to help. Notice the bow ties on the grounds crew.

Abner Powell, owner and manager of the 1887 New Orleans Pelicans, got the idea to use a tarpaulin to cover the infield during rainstorms by watching stevedores on the docks use tarpaulins to protect the cotton bales. The next year, during spring training, the Cincinnati Reds watched the Pelican ground crew cover the playing surface with a tarpaulin. They carried the idea back to the National League, where it became standard practice. Over time the tarps became greased with oil or paraffin to enhance their water resistance. Powell invented a rain check to use when the tarpaulin did not work.

During the 1890s most clubs stored the oily tarpaulins under the grandstand until a series of ballpark fires in 1894 led the National League to suspect a "fire bug." However, closer investigation showed that fans in the grandstands discarded used, but still lit, cigars by tossing them. Invariably the lit cigars landed on the oily tarps and only a downpour from the skies could save the park.

The invention and use of the rain tarp meant that baseball men could sometimes fool Mother Nature. Just as today, families in the early days also travelled many miles to watch big league baseball games. Sudden spring showers could put the park out of commission. The tarpaulins enabled clubs to play most of their scheduled games.

The First Press Passes
A Nod to the Sportswriter

1908

RIGHT: The 1945 New York Baseball Writers Dinner, annually hosted by Toots Shor, featured sportswriters, players and front office personnel.
BOTTOM: The 1911 World Series press box was open and in plain view of the players and fans.

The Baseball Writers Association of America (BBWAA) had turbulent beginnings in 1908 when Hugh Fullerton, unable to find a seat in the press section of the Polo Grounds during the playoff game, sat on the lap of Broadway actor Louis Mann, who claimed his seat had been given him by Giants manager John J. McGraw. The insult of an actor in the press box, and the slight at the 1908 World Series when sportswriters were expected to climb onto the roof of old Bennett Park in icy September weather to cover the games, convinced Joseph Jackson of the *Detroit Free Press* to lead the movement to establish the BBWAA. Its objectives were: give the press box to the writer, make sense out of the scoring rules, and champion the square deal in baseball. The infant organization became powerful in 1911 when the two New York clubs, the Highlanders and Giants, refused press box admission to anyone not showing a BBWAA membership card. The organization of today has maintained a prestigious position in baseball, voting annually for Hall of Fame members, as well as many postseason awards, including the Most Valuable Player and Cy Young awards.

World S

The First Moveable Fences
Field of Nightmares

1895

Many baseball fans remembered fondly the days of 1961 when Athletics owner Charles O. Finley built his moveable fence. The idea focused on the fact that the New York Yankees won 27 pennants from 1923 through 1964, using the 296-foot right field porch. Finley installed a barrier that cut across the outfield until it reached the right field foul pole 296 feet from home plate. He called the area behind the barrier his "Pennant Porch." Baseball Commissioner Ford Frick and AL President Joe Cronin ordered him to remove it or forfeit his home games. The following season, he extended a roof over the field to the 296-foot mark, claiming that fans in the stands needed shade. This time, supervisor of umpires Cal Hubbard ordered him to remove the portion that extended onto the field. Finley was not the first owner who tried to manipulate the fences for his advantage.

Charles Comiskey owned the St. Paul Apostles in 1895. He wanted his first ball club to win so he stocked it with ex-major leaguers and constructed a moveable fence which was brought in when his club hit, and pushed back when the opposing team came to the plate. The experiment failed to pass the approval of Western League president Ban Johnson, but the ploy impressed Johnson enough that he courted Comiskey for his grandiose plans to found a new major league at the turn of the century.

The First Club to Paint
the Center Field Wall Black
Only the Wall was White

1895

The 1896 Cincinnati club improved after painting their center field wall black for better ball visibility. Baseball has always been innovative and responsive to new ideas.

Sunday-best white shirts posed a problematic background for 1895 batters trying to pick up the flight of the baseball when it left the pitcher's hand. Erstwhile .300 hitter Bug Holliday complained to the Cincinnati club officials that he couldn't see the ball. They replied that nobody could see the ball coming out of the pitcher's hand on a Sunday when the center field bleachers were full. The Sunday crowds, which numbered 15,000, paid the bills for the weekday forays that barely drew 3,000.

The club proposed a compromise. They'd paint the center wall black. An interesting thing happened. The Reds' batters cut down on strikes and kept their high batting averages, but power hitting dwindled while their pitching staff adapted to the background by lowering the team ERA more than two runs per game and increasing strikeouts. Cincy improved so much that they finished third in 1896.

The First Ballpark with Synthetic Turf

Eighth Wonder of the World

1966

The Houston Astrodome became baseball's first ballpark with synthetic turf in 1966. This photo shows a Cubs 4–3 win over the hometown Astros 20 years later, on August 23, 1986.

The air-conditioned Astrodome opened April 9, 1965, with an exhibition game between the New York Yankees and Houston Astros. The Yankees batted Mickey Mantle, who hit the first home run, in the leadoff spot so that he would be the first to bat in the new stadium.

Billed as the Eighth Wonder of the World, the domed stadium cost Harris County taxpayers $31,600,000, but had a glaring problem. Sunlight poured through the porous dome and blinded fielders trying to catch fly balls. The Astros painted the outside of the dome to prevent sunlight from coming in. It worked, but it also killed the grass.

After a year of trying to grow grass, Monsanto offered a synthetic grass to Harris County officials. Major League Baseball approved of the new technology and artificial turf was adapted for baseball use in 1966. Lacking a name for it, fans, sportswriters and chemists called the synthetic grass "Astroturf."

Uniforms

The First Team Uniforms
Now Wearing a Cunning Flannel Bodice

1849

Alexander Cartwright, top middle, is surrounded by the nattily-dressed members of the Knickerbocker Base Ball Club.

The New York Knickerbockers adopted a uniform, on April 24, 1849, consisting of blue woolen pantaloons, white flannel shirt and straw hat. The wearing of similar uniforms changed the game from an exercise to a fashion contest between competing teams. At first the color of the socks mattered most.

Teams today are still identified by the socks they wore more than 100 years ago. The Chicago White Sox, Boston Red Sox, Cincinnati Reds and the Detroit Tigers, who wore vertical striped socks, have retained nicknames related to sock color.

An interesting experiment with colored uniforms took place in 1882. The National League authorized uniforms for each position; the only difference from club to club would be the color of their socks. The colors adopted were white for Chicago, dark blue for Cleveland, light blue for Providence, brown for Worcester, gray for Buffalo, green for Troy, red for Boston and yellow for Detroit. The uniform shirt, belt and cap colors by position were scarlet and white for first base, orange and blue for second base, blue and white for third base, maroon for shortstop, white for left field, red and black for center field, gray for right field, light blue for pitcher, scarlet for catcher, and green and brown for substitutes. All pants and ties were white, and all shoes leather. When the league found that blue and white materials for the third sacker were unavailable they switched to gray and white. In July the league abandoned colored shirts for various positions. The experiment had been called "clownish" by the papers.

The First Uniform Numbers
Count on It!

1916

Miller Huggins managed the Yankees in 1929 — the year the team first wore numbers on their backs — until his untimely mid-season death. Here he watches practice with front office personnel.

Jack Graney, leadoff batter for the Cleveland Naps in 1916, wore a miniscule number one on his sleeve. The numbers proved to be less than exciting so they were discontinued the following season. The popular New York Yankees saw an increasing number of new fans pouring into their stadium. Most could not identify the player by sight. In a bold move, the Yankee introduced numbers in 1929, but instead of small and unobtrusive, they made them big and plastered them on the players' backs. The original numbering system copied the batting order, Ruth #3, Gehrig #4, and so forth. By 1932 all big league teams wore numbers. The Dodgers of 1952 repeated numbers on the front. Some clubs picked this innovation up, but the practice did not become universal.

Another idea that did become universal sprouted from the fertile mind of Bill Veeck. In 1960, the same year he introduced the exploding scoreboard, he placed names on the back of the White Sox uniforms. Within a short time, almost every club overcame its fears of lost scorecard revenue to stitch their players' names on the back of the uniforms.

The First Team to Wear Short Pants
The Bees' Knees!

1950

Never short on ideas, White Sox owner Bill Veeck persuaded retired Sox player Jim Rivera to model the new hot-weather home uniforms of the 1976 Chicago team.

The All-American Girls Professional Baseball League players wore skirts and did not hurt themselves too much. So why couldn't male baseball players wear shorts?

The independently owned Hollywood Stars competed in the Pacific Coast League against teams from larger cities such as Los Angeles, San Francisco and San Diego. They needed more of a drawing card than a weekly mention on *The Jack Benny Show*.

On April 1, 1950, the Hollywood Stars appeared on the playing field wearing short pants, marking the first time such attire had ever been worn in a regular Organized Baseball contest. The idea originated with Fred Haney, manager of the Hollywood club. The next year the club went back to full length trousers, but the attendance dropped 150,000 and they lost their affiliation with Brooklyn.

The 1975 White Sox suffered at the gate and on the playing field. New owner Bill Veeck dressed the following year's players in short pants. They still did poorly the diamond, but the attendance improved 22 percent. The following year the club got better and quit wearing short pants.

The First Double-knit Uniforms
Stylish Pirates

1970

Dave Parker looked big
and menacing to pitchers
in any uniform. Here he
sports the stylish double-
knit look introduced by
the Pirates in 1970.

The Pittsburgh Pirates introduced the beltless double-knit
uniform to the majors in 1970. They kept their wool and
cotton blend belted model just in case, but the new era
had arrived. The next year the Astros and Cardinals wore
the new duds while the American League Orioles casually introduced them to the home crowd. The next year they would go
fully double-knit.

By 1975 only Chicago and New York in the American
League did not sport the "new" look. In the Senior Circuit, only
half of the 12 teams wore double-knits. The new form-fitting
uniforms attracted more attention from the female fans, who
doubtless enjoyed the new view.

The First Player to Wear his Birthday on his Back
Birthday Suit

1968

Carlos May was excited when he heard that he was going up to the big leagues from Lynchburg in the Carolina League. He knew that the White Sox featured uniforms with players' names on the back. He had a boyhood dream of someday wearing his birthday, May 17, on the back of his uniform.

When he came up in 1968, May stuck with the big league Sox and won the American League Rookie of the Year for 1969. And he did it as May 17. That marvelous piece of personal advertising didn't miss Charles Finley, owner of the Kansas City Athletics.

Finley was his own scouting department, his own publicity director, his own stadium architect, and his own pat on the back. Finley was the man who sold liability insurance to doctors during the 1950s, and he believed that the player uniform was an overlooked opportunity for promotion. He tried to talk Vida Blue into changing his first name to True. He convinced John Odom that he had a better chance to stick in the big leagues if he had a catchy nickname like Catfish Hunter. Finley and Odom agreed on Blue Moon. Sportswriters complain that there are no more colorful nicknames in baseball. Well, there are no more owners like Charles Finley.

The First Player to Alter his Uniform
Dazzling Pitches

1924

BELOW: An aging Dazzy Vance shows, in 1932, the uniform sleeves that the NL rule makers forced upon him. That is, no frayed sleeves.

BELOW RIGHT: In the 1950s, the Reds' Ted Kluszewski cut off his sleeves to fit his bulging arm muscles.

Dazzy Vance was a career minor leaguer with only flashes of brilliance to show for it when he was called up by Brooklyn in 1922. After two so-so years, he altered his uniform. The big right-hander slit his undershirt sleeve on his pitching arm to give the ball the appearance of exploding out of a haze of flapping strings. As the 1924 season progressed he took to tying small knots in the strings. Doubling his 1922 strikeout total, Vance cut more than a run off his ERA and won 28 as the Dodgers missed the pennant by a game and a half. As a result of Vance's sensational year, pitchers were forbidden to alter their uniforms, but not so with batters.

Cincinnati fans remembered the 1950s when big Klu (Ted Kluszewski) cut out his sleeves to show his bulging muscles. Four decades later outfielder Deion Sanders appeared in uniform with his sleeves cut and his socks pulled high to his knees. Encountering protest from Major League Baseball, which forbade altering of the uniform without permission because it might affect licensing revenues, several members of the Reds cut off their sleeves in solidarity with Sanders and to adhere to the rule that all uniforms must be similar. Sanders claimed that he was honoring the Negro League players, but he probably wanted to make a fashion statement.

Equipment

The First Player and First Catcher to Use Shinguards
Why Suffer?

1880s
1907

TOP LEFT: Bud Fowler (top middle) and other African-American second basemen wore wooden slats under their socks during the nineteenth century.

TOP RIGHT: A well-padded Roger Bresnahan demonstrated the turn-of-the-century catching technique that left the shins vulnerable to foul tips.

Roger Bresnahan, the multi-talented catcher for the New York Giants at the turn of the century, started his career as a pitcher. He sometimes batted second or leadoff, and he managed for the first female owner of the twentieth century, Helene Britton Robison. He was also elected to the Baseball Hall of Fame over his contemporary, Johnny Kling, because he was an innovator as well as a ballplayer. Bresnahan wore a pneumatic batting helmet to spring training in 1906. He carried shinguards with him in 1907. The helmet did not work but the shinguards did. They were modeled after cricket leg guards; the first ones were bulky with a knee flap that came up to the thigh. Although shinguards were initially met with ridicule and protest, they became popular by 1909 when they adopted a smaller, more utilitarian size and shape. Bresnahan was likely aware of previous shinguards used by an African-American second baseman through his close association with Manager John McGraw, who conversed with future Negro League founder Rube Foster and scouted black second sacker Charlie Grant for Baltimore in the American League.

Bud Fowler and Sol White, both African-American infielders, were known to stuff their long socks with wooden slats during the 1880s to protect their bones from the spikes of sliding baserunners who were trying to break up double plays or just cut the black players. Fowler toiled 10 years in Organized Ball minor leagues as part of 27-year professional career. His guards served a needed purpose the same as Bresnahan's did 20 years later.

The First Cork-centered Baseball
The Lively Ball

1910

Ben Shibe (middle) and
Al Reach (right) discuss
business while attending
a ball game in the early
1920s. Shibe and Reach
were partners who intro-
duced the lively cork-
centered baseball that rev-
olutionized the game.

The first baseballs were hand-made. The Knickerbockers hired a Scottish saddle maker to stitch the cover over rubber cuttings wound with yarn. The outer cover kept coming loose and the fielders could not throw it very far, which necessitated the shortstop helping with relays. In 1871 Benjamin Shibe and his brother organized his leather company, which held the patent on the figure-eight ball cover. The design replaced the old lemon-peel baseball of the 1860s. One problem still existed, however.

The India-rubber in the center of the ball could be manipulated by heating or cooling it. Connie Mack, later the 50-year manager of the Philadelphia A's, once led the National League Pittsburgh Pirates. He installed an old refrigerator unit in his office that was used to freeze baseballs to make them dead before the ball boys handed them to the umpires for games. After the turn of the century, the baseballs and the National Pastime became dead. League officials, seeking to put more offense into the game, listened attentively to Ben Shibe's proposal to use his new cork-centered ball. The manufactured balls had a lighter cork center rather than the rubber one. To adjust the weight more wrappings were needed, resulting in harder, denser baseballs. The ball would fly farther when struck. The American League adopted the new Reach — manufactured by Shibe — for play in 1910.

One more innovation lay ahead for the baseball. In 1920 ball makers discovered that Australian wool could be stretched and wound tighter than our American wool. The tighter ball, abandonment of trick pitches and widespread use of shaved-handle bats led to the "Big Bang" era that is more commonly known as the Lively Ball era. The improvement in equipment gave the National Pastime more action and more home runs. The increase in long-ball hitting thrilled fans, who flocked to the ballparks to spend stock market gains at America's favorite activity — cheering for winners.

The First Player to Wear Leg Weights in Spring Training

Cobb had a Leg Up

1910s

In this often-used photograph Ty Cobb uses his fadeway or hook slide to evade the tag. The Georgia Peach developed his speed with the innovative use of leg weights during spring training in the 1910s.

The Immortal Georgia Peach arrived in the major leagues in 1905 with a chip on his southern shoulder and an imperative from his father. "Come home a success or don't come home at all," his clearly disappointed father had told the young ballplayer. Tragedy awaited the Cobb family.

During Cobb's first season in Detroit, his mother shot his father, thinking that he was an intruder at his home. The distraught Cobb did not attend the funeral. Instead he drove himself to be one of the greatest players who ever lived. That next spring, when he showed up determined to be the best, one of his training devices was leaded shoes.

Through spring training — although Cobb's attendance was spotty, since he hated playing exhibition games for which he did not get paid — the erstwhile sprinter from Georgia ran and ran, but he seemed slower than usual. He wore lead weights in his shoes. When the season started he replaced the training shoes with his regular spikes. His feet and legs felt light as feathers, and the speedy Cobb ran as though he were flying through the air. His opponents saw him as a whirling dervish, a flashy blur on the basepaths. The effect of Cobb's training technique made him the most feared baserunner in the American League. The leg weights gave him a tremendous psychological advantage that was based in physical superiority.

The First Player to Use a Donut Bat Weight

Ellie the Inventor

1968

Elston Howard looks at the bat weight donut that he invented and used during 1968 spring training, near the end of his ballplaying career.

Casey Stengel, Elston Howard's manager with the New York Yankees, laughingly complained that he and the Yankees waited many years for a black player, and when they got one, he was the only African-American who couldn't steal bases. But Stengel knew he had acquired a heady, winning ballplayer.

Ellie Howard became Whitey Ford's special catcher. Trained in the old Negro Leagues — a league that never outlawed trick pitches — Howard showed Ford how to load his famed cut fastball by scraping the horsehide on a sharpened shinguard buckle. Ford won 25 and lost only four in 1961 when Howard became the full-time Yankee receiver. Howard made other contributions as a hitter.

He watched on-deck hitters loosen up by trying to time pitches while swinging two or three bats. The use of multiple bats created the effect of warming up with a heavy stick — Babe Ruth had used a special 48-ounce war club — then switching to a lighter stick. Howard thought, "Why switch bats? Why grip three bats instead of your regular bat?" He had a weight made that slipped over the knob and slid down to the business end of the bat. He called it a donut because it was round with a hole in it. After several years the donut became a regular piece of equipment for all ball clubs.

Howard proved that ballplayers were no dummies. The effect of an active ballplayer inventing something that improved the game showed other players that baseball was a thinking man's game.

The First Catcher to Use a Turkey Neck
Necessity!

1970s

Dodger catcher Steve Yeager developed the protective turkey neck, seen here attached to his mask, in the 1970s.

Catching gear was often called the "Tools of Ignorance." Before gloves were used, nineteenth-century receivers warmed up for the season by laying their hands on barrels of sand and allowing the team to beat on their hands with baseball bats. No wonder catchers were considered odd. Mashed fingers and smashed Adam's apples were considered hazards of the position. Professional catchers routinely suffered from foul tips, but blows on the Adam's apple could actually injure the receiver for life.

Steve Yeager, the catcher for the Los Angeles Dodgers of the 1970s, thought surely there must be a better method for protecting catchers from vicious foul balls that came straight back. He experimented with different devices and settled for a piece of hard plastic that hung down from the mask. It looked like the flap that hung down from a turkey's beak. Yeager called his protective device a "turkey neck."

Like the catcher's mask 100 years earlier, the advantage of the turkey neck was recognized immediately. Catchers contacted the Dodgers and Yeager about ordering them. Once again, a ballplayer had invented a device that improved his profession.

The First Player to Use a Cupped Bat
It Came from Kyoto

1971

Jose Cardenal joined the Cardinals in March of 1970. Known for his idiosyncrasies, Cardenal used his inventive mind to adapt the cupped bat to the majors.

Jose Cardenal, a career .275 hitter with 18 years in the big leagues, may never make the Hall of Fame, but many future Hall of Famers have him to thank for introducing the cupped-end bat to the majors.

Cardenal, in-law of Bert Campaneris and reputed tough character, left the Cardinals with more than they ever imagined in a mid-season trade with Milwaukee in 1971. He had brought a cupped bat to the Cardinals from Japan where he'd picked it up during a short visit. Cardenal used the bat and discussed the concept with Cardinals leadoff batter Lou Brock. Major League Baseball approved of the bat and Brock began to use the cupped bat in games. His career took off.

Brock, who had batted .300 only once before using the cupped bat, averaged .306 for seven years following his introduction of the Japanese model. His bat speed increased, his on-base percentage rose and he made the All-Star team in four of the first five years after switching to the cupped bat.

The First Pitching Machines
Ol' Pete

1896

Early pitching machines were called "Ol' Pete" after Grover Cleveland Alexander, who had better control than the batting practice devices. Of his 373 career wins (3rd all-time), 90 were shutouts (2nd all-time).

Professor Charles Hinton of Princeton University demonstrated his patented pitching machine in 1896. It resembled a short, breech-loading cannon, mounted on a two-wheeled carriage. Its bore was not rifled but smooth. A curve could be produced by manipulating the prongs which protruded from the cannon's mouth and against which the ball rubbed in passing, acquiring the rotary motion which caused the curve. By adjusting the prongs an in-curve, out-curve, upshoot, or drop could result. The speed of the ball depended upon the amount of powder placed in the cartridge.

While the machine did not last, the idea stayed around. By the 1930s every club had a pitching machine for spring training. Most of the machines were called "Ol' Pete" after Grover Cleveland Alexander. Batters noticed that the machine poured ball after ball over the plate in the strike zone. Pitching in tiny Baker Bowl, Alexander lived on the outside corner, seldom giving a batsman any pitch that he could pull. Alexander also had remarkable control, issuing only 951 bases on balls in 5,190 innings. His opponents' on-base percentage was .288, despite the fact that he pitched during the lively ball era.

The First Team to Use Training Facilities
Y-M-C-A

1879

The 1878 Buffalo Bisons — depicted on a trading card — won the International Association pennant and gained acceptance into the NL after training at the YMCA facilities.

The 1878 Buffalo Bisons won the pennant in the International Association. Their lineup featured several Clipper Prize (all-star) winners, enticing the National League to invite the club to join them for the 1879 season. The excited Buffalo directors readily accepted, but worried about their preparedness for daily play against the best professionals in the world. The Bison directors came up with an unusual idea.

Buffalo team officials approached the local YMCA about using their facilities for training. The YMCA director agreed, but insisted that first each member of the Bisons had to join the "Y." Reluctantly, Buffalo signed up the nucleus of their first National League club.

While the Buffalo players worked out in a first class gymnasium during the winter of 1878-79, the YMCA was busy advertising, nationally, the availability of training facilities to build tough men. "Even the champions of the International Association used the facilities," bragged the YMCA publicity. Response generated from the Buffalo Bisons' use of the local gym started a national movement for the "Y." After the Bisons trained there, the YMCAs outshone rival athletic clubs.

The First Player to Wear Sunglasses
Smoked Glass

1880s

aul Hines, a deaf outfielder who played more than 20 years, was thought to be the originator of the sunglasses. He used them in the 1880s, but they needed improvement. Fred Clarke, the Pittsburgh Pirate outfielder and manager who began his Hall of Fame career with a 5-for-5 performance, spent years and much money at the turn of the century trying to patent smoked glass sunglasses, or to interest Corning Glass in his prototype. Clarke also introduced flip-down sunglasses.

There is a famous photo of Casey Stengel wearing small granny-like sunglasses. Stengel and Clarke were friends, despite their age difference, because of their common interest in innovation in Kansas City during the off-season. Clarke may have enticed Stengel to use the glasses during the 1916 season.

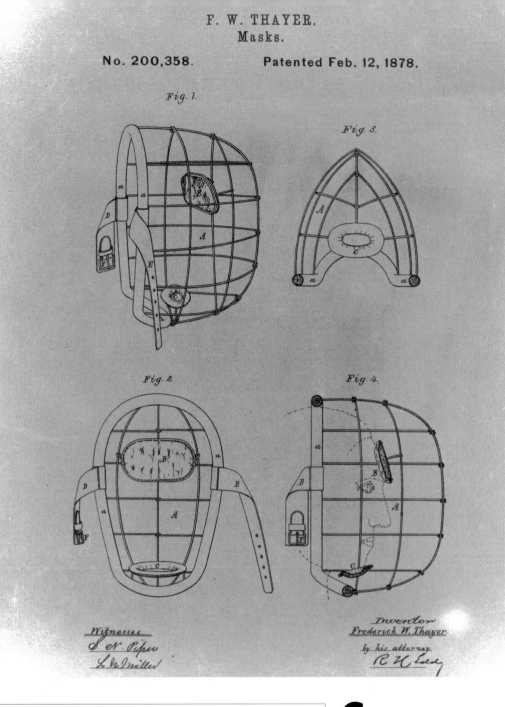

F. W. THAYER.
Masks.

No. 200,358.   Patented Feb. 12, 1878.

Fig. 1.

Fig. 3.

Fig. 2.

Fig. 4.

Witnesses
J. N. Piper
L. W. Miller

Inventor
Frederick W. Thayer.
by his attorney
R. H. Eddy

The First Catcher to Use a Face Mask

A Harvard Legacy

1877

Fred Thayer's patent application was filed after he discovered plans by Spalding and Company to mass produce catcher's masks for the 1878 season. Spalding replaced the flimsy wire cage with one of sturdy steel alloy.

Sometimes, an idea occurred that was so good that it was universally accepted immediately upon its introduction. The catcher's mask was such an invention.

Invented by Fred Thayer, captain of the Harvard University nine, the first catcher's mask was a fencing mask with eye holes cut into the wire mesh. Thayer's teammate and catcher James Tyng, who played seven years for Harvard and may have been the best baseball player ever to wear the Crimson, placed the contraption over his head for a game against the Lynn Live Oaks Base Ball Club — an International Association team — on April 11, 1877. Harvard proved its influence among baseball nines by seeing some form of Thayer's mask in universal use before the season concluded. During Thayer's years Harvard played several professional teams, even beating two National League squads. Thayer claimed as his justification for the miracle invention, "Tyng was the best all-around natural ballplayer of my time, but he had been hit by foul tips and had become more or less timid."

The mask was patented in 1878, by which time Spalding was producing it as part of its equipment catalog. By mid-season in 1878 every catcher in the world was utilizing Thayer's invention and Spalding's innovation.

The First Player to Wear a Batting Helmet

Beanball Wars

1905

BELOW: Willie Wells first wore a miner's helmet to protect against beanballs in the Negro Leagues in 1939.
BELOW RIGHT: Beanball wars almost claimed Joe Medwick as a 1941 casualty.

I n 1905 the Reach Sporting Goods Company patented a pneumatic batting helmet. It was worn in spring training by Roger Bresnahan, who found it too bulky to use in league games. The helmet resembled a leather football headpiece with half cut away. The left ear flap covered the left temple for right-handed batters and the right ear flap was for left-handed swingers. Beanballs were frequent, and even after Cleveland shortstop Ray Chapman was killed by a beaning in 1920, the idea of batting helmets still did not take hold.

Willie Wells, Negro League Hall of Fame shortstop, crowded the plate in a batting style that hung his head over the plate in the strike zone. He also was a heavy hitter , which encouraged pitchers to throw at him. In 1939 during a beanball flap Wells donned a miner's helmet. Three years later he went to a New Jersey construction site and borrowed a hardhat which he modified into a batting helmet. Meanwhile a criminal beaning occurred in the National League.

Joe Medwick had been traded from the Cardinals to the Dodgers in 1940. Following an altercation between Medwick, Leo Durocher, and rival pitcher Bob Bowman in an elevator in the morning, Medwick was beaned by ex-teammate Bowman. The incident caused Dodger owner Larry MacPhail to rush onto the field and verbally attack the coaches in the Cardinals' dugout. The New York attorney general investigated the matter as attempted murder. Dodger batters PeeWee Reese and Joe Medwick used helmet inserts after near-fatal beanings.

The first club to provide batting helmets for all of its players was the 1952 Pirates. General Manager Branch Rickey tried the novel idea of bringing up rookies to the majors to let them learn baseball at the big league level. He worried about their ability to duck high inside pitches. The helmet idea caught on. Now all batters in the majors use ear flap helmets, a concept that would have caused them to be laughed them off the field 50 years earlier.

THE GAME

T his section highlights the "game" aspect of our National Pastime. Great performances, scoring, fans, sportswriters and travel are elements that make the game come alive. Baseball is more than a contest between two sets of nine. "Hope springs eternal in the human breast" is a line from *Casey at the Bat,* and it represents the fundamental attraction of our National Pastime. Hope for something better. A hitter hopes that the next at-bat will be better than the last. A pitcher hopes that the next batter will be easier than the previous one. All losers hope that tomorrow will bring victory and all winners hope that the next game will have the same result. The essence of baseball is portrayed in that one poem. But Casey and William DeWolff Hopper were infants when the National Pastime started.

No man was more important to the development of baseball — its rules, its statistics and its reporting — than Henry Chadwick. Born in England in 1824, he came to the United States at age 13 steeped in the tradition of cricket. In his teens he played the English game, and in his twenties he reported on it for a variety of newspapers, including the *Long Island Star* and the *New York Times.* In the early 1840s, before the Knickerbocker rules eliminated the practice of retiring baserunners by hitting them with a thrown ball, Chadwick occasionally played baseball, but was not favorably impressed, having received "some hard hits in the ribs."

Chadwick became won over to the baseball side when returning from a cricket match on Fox Hill; he went through the Elysian Fields during a contest between the Eagle and Gotham baseball clubs. The game was being sharply played on both sides, and he was struck with the idea that baseball was the game for a national sport for Americans, just as cricket was in England. He had already developed a system of reporting cricket matches in box score format.

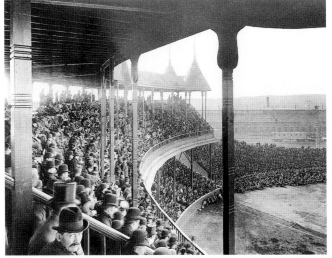

LEFT: Baseball at twilight. **BELOW**: Fans pack the stands of Boston's Grand Pavilion at the South End Grounds for a nineteenth-century game.

Chadwick's ideas developed into the baseball box score. His summary of the season in statistical formats appeared in the leading sports publications of the day, *New York Clipper* and Beadle's *Dime Base-Ball Player.* He discovered that Americans devoured news in daily publications. Chadwick knew what newspapers throughout the country learned during the nineteenth century: baseball was a ready source of daily, exciting and unpredictable news.

Let's read the why and the what of the daily news of baseball, from Chadwick's first box scores, to the first night game, to the first teams to travel around the world, and beyond.

Scoring and Rules

The First Box Score
The Lure of Stats

1845

TOP: *The Ball Players' Chronicle* was edited by Henry Chadwick in 1867. This write-up features an early box score.
BOTTOM: Henry Chadwick, who recognized the importance of statistics, was the first writer to see baseball as the "National Game" for Americans.

The first box score appeared in the *New York Morning News* on October 22, 1845, less than a month after Alexander Cartwright and his Knickerbocker teammates codified the first set of rules. Why the connection between the game and statistics in newsprint at this very early — indeed the earliest — stage of baseball's history is answered by John Thorn in *Total Baseball.* He wrote that the box score was devised "in part to imitate the custom of cricket, yet the larger explanation is that the numbers served to legitimize men's concern with a boys' pastime." The pioneers of baseball reporting — William Cauldwell of the *Sunday Mercury,* William Porter of the *Spirit of the Times,* the unknown analyst at the *News,* and later Henry Chadwick — may indeed have reflected that if they did not cloak the game in the "importance" of statistics, it might not seem worthwhile for adults to read about, let alone play.

Statistics elevated baseball from other boys' games of the 1840s and 1850s to make it somehow systematic and serious, like a business. That business was selling papers for the publishing companies. They quickly learned sports and baseball scores in particular sold newspapers. Many nineteenth-century productions consisted of four pages. The front was national, political and serious local news. The inside was local and gossip or installments of a spicy book or sensuous affair. (Sex sold in the old days just like today. The hottest story of 1877 was of Rev. Henry Ward Beecher — the greatest Evangelist of the day — and his adulterous relationship with his secretary.) A financial page and sports page finished the daily news report. Newspapers sought baseball and not vice-versa, because baseball was daily news. No other source of happy, agreeable news would ever be found that was as easily to access as baseball.

Interestingly, early box scores did not register hits. The batting champion was the player who scored the most runs per game. A player's performance was also measured by the number of outs he committed. The term "hands out" balanced outs against runs in the first box scores. The assumption was that once on base the runner should run until he scored or a putout was recorded.

The First Codified Playing Rules
You Could Look it Up

1845

At the dawn of baseball Henry Cartwright suggested that the Knickerbockers, who had been playing informally since at least 1842, be organized as a club with a constitution and playing rules. He then, with other club members, drafted the original 14 playing rules. These rules were first used for a match between the Knickerbockers and the New York nine on June 19, 1846. They were:

1. The bases shall be from "home" to second base, 42 paces; from first to third base, 42 paces — equidistant.

2. The game to consist of 21 counts or aces, but at the conclusion an equal number of hands must be played.

3. The ball must be pitched, and not thrown, for the bat.

4. A ball knocked outside the range of the first or third base, is foul.

5. Three balls being struck at and missed and the last one caught is a hand out; if not caught, is considered fair; the striker bound to run.

6. A ball being struck or tipped and caught either flying or on the first bound is a hand out.

7. A player, running the bases, shall be out if the ball is in the hands of an adversary on the base, or the runner is touched by it before he makes his base; it being understood, however, that in no instance is a ball to be thrown at him.

8. A player running, who shall prevent an adversary from catching or getting the ball before making his base, is a hand out.

9. If two hands are already out a player running home at the time a ball is struck, cannot make an ace if the striker is caught out.

10. Three hands out, all out.

11. Players must take their strike in regular turn.

12. No ace or base can be made on a foul strike.

13. A runner cannot be put out in making one base when a balk is made by the pitcher.

14. But one base allowed when the ball bounds out of the field when struck.

THE RULES A CENTURY AGO

Fortunately the rules under which the great game was played have been preserved. These rules were devised in 1845 by the Knickerbockers.

(Words in parentheses are for editorial explanation)

Sec. 1—The Bases shall be from "home" to second base 42 paces: from first to third base 42 paces equidistant.

Sec. 2—The game to consist of 21 counts or aces (runs), but at the conclusion an equal number of hands (outs) must be played.

Sec. 3—The ball must be pitched (underhand) and not thrown (freehand) for the bat.

Sec. 4—A ball knocked outside the range of first or third is foul. (If it hit inside but rolled out it was fair.)

Sec. 5—Three balls being struck at and missed and the last one caught is a hand (player) out: if not caught is considered fair and the striker bound to run.

Sec. 6—A ball being struck or tipped and caught either flying or on the first bounce is a hand out.

Sec. 7—A player running the bases shall be out if the ball is in the hands of an adversary and the runner is touched by it before he makes his base, it being understood, however, that in no instance is the ball to be thrown at him. (He could also be forced out at bases.)

Sec. 8—A player running who shall prevent an adversary from catching or getting the ball before making his base is a hand out.

Sec. 9—If two hands are already out, a player running home at the time a ball is struck cannot make an ace if the striker is thrown out.

Sec. 10—Three hands out, all out.

Sec. 11—Players must take their strike in regular turn.

Sec. 12—No ace or base shall be made on a foul strike.

Sec. 13—A runner cannot be put out in making one base when a balk is made by the pitcher.

Sec. 14—But one base allowed when the ball bounds out of the field when struck.

Notable among these rules — which simply codified the game that the Knicks were already playing — were the laying out of the baseball on a "diamond" rather than a square, the concept of foul territory, and the elimination of retiring a runner by hitting him with the ball. These were critical differences from earlier games, sufficient in and of themselves to term the Knickerbocker rules a landmark in the evolution of baseball.

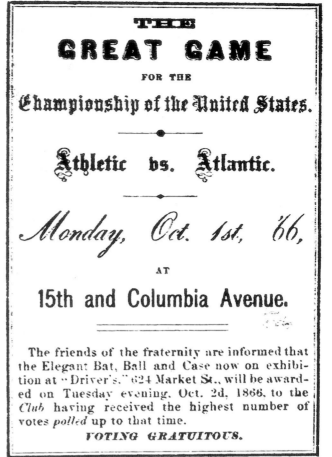

The First Scorecard
The Fans' Friend

1845

TOP: One of the earliest printed scorecards touted the Championship Series of 1866.

RIGHT: An early souvenir scorecard for the Temple Cup NL Championship Series between New York and Baltimore.

Before the first enclosed ball field, club owners were already hawking scorecards for additional income. The earliest known scorecard, located at the New York Public Library, revealed a game played on October 6, 1845. It was a pre-printed Knickerbocker Ball Club card. The categories were names, hands out, runs, and remarks. Other scorecards followed as the idea was a good one.

During the first year of the National Association, Mort Rogers — old-time Philly ballplayer — produced beautiful, sometimes hand-colored, printed scorecards. They made big hits in Philadelphia, Boston and New York, where they featured the daguerreotype of a local player on the front. Earlier than 1871, a special scorecard was printed for the October 1, 1866, game between the Philadelphia Athletics and the Brooklyn Atlantics. The game drew the largest crowd of the nineteenth century, as more than 30,000 fans tried to get into the Philly ballpark. Spillage onto the playing field rendered the contest undoable. The two teams tried again October 15 and doubled the admission to 50 cents, but still drew 18,000. There was no record as to how many scorecards were sold, but one still exists at the Baseball Hall of Fame.

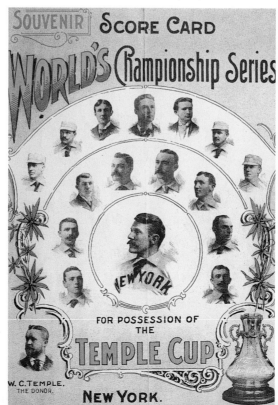

The First Balls and Strikes

Steee-rike One!

1863

An umpired game at Bates College in 1882. The calling of balls and strikes may have been the result of batters being afraid to swing at increasingly swift pitches.

The first calling of balls and strikes occurred at the start of the 1863 season, but only to prevent the purposeful delay of the game. The calling of strikes appeared in the first codified rules. Number 11 of the 1845 Knickerbocker Base Ball Club rules read: "Three balls being struck at and missed and the last one caught, is a hand out; if not caught is considered fair, and the striker (batter) bound to run."

Later, in 1857, the ball clubs of the National Association of Base Ball Players adopted a 35-point code that included two provisions for strikeouts. One called the striker out if the catcher caught the third strike, the other declared the striker a runner if the catcher failed to snag the third strike.

The next year (1858) the official playing rules were amended to include a strike zone definition. The rules read: "Should a striker stand at the bat without striking at good balls repeatedly pitched to him, for the purpose of delaying the game or of giving advantage to a player, the umpire, after warning him, shall call one strike, and if he persists in such action, two and three strikes. When three strikes are called, he shall be subject to the same rules as if he had struck at the three balls."

Strike zones originally included any pitch that the striker could reach with a bat. Through the years they became refined and further defined until today's skimpy model. Allowing the umpires to call strikes gave them control of the game and eventually led to paid umpire staffs and a code of professional conduct. Moreover, the calling of balls and strikes turned the game into a medieval joust between a pitcher and batter, one knight armed with a ball and the other with a bat. The spirited contest lasted one second, but it was repeated more than 100 times for each side. The called strike took away the emphasis on fielding and placed it at home plate and on the pitcher and catcher.

The First Infield Fly Rule
I Got it, I Got it!

1895

Taking advantage in the days before the infield fly rule, shortstop George Wright routinely dropped fly balls so he could turn double plays. Wright played on nine championship clubs in 11 years.

According to legend, shortstop George Wright of Cincinnati and Boston routinely dropped short fly balls with runners on base so that he could throw to the bases ahead of them for two force outs instead of the one fly out. The infield fly rule was established in 1895, long after Wright's career was over, allowing umpires to call outs on infield fly balls whether or not they were caught.

The infield fly rule plays a role in the most confusing play of a hypothetical game. A player could have gotten credit for a triple play but never have touched the ball. This is how it could happen. An infield fly was hit near second base. The umpire called the batter out; the runner on first was running on the pitch and passed the runner on second, who wandered off the bag, but held up due to the shortstop camped under the pop fly. A gust of wind took the pop-up away from the shortstop and dropped on the head of the runner who was supposed to be on second base and who was just passed by the runner from first base. The batter was out according to the infield fly rule. The first baserunner was out for passing a runner in the basepaths. The third out was registered when the runner was hit by a batted ball. All putouts went to the nearest defensive player. Since shortstop was nearest and the original caller for the pop fly, he got credit for all three outs, but never touched the ball.

The infield fly rule prevented a team from cheating. The baseball rules were set up like the game of life. There were some good rules and some that made no sense. Players tried follow them, they tried to circumvent them, they disputed them and they fought over them so much that an impartial observer was designated as the keeper of the rules. In baseball the rules are the game.

The First President to Throw Out the First Pitch
Executive Privilege

1910

TOP: President William
H. Taft throws out the first
pitch in 1910.
BOTTOM: Hillary Rodham
Clinton grew up a Cubs fan.
As First Lady she winged the
opening pitch of the 1994
season at Wrigley Field.

U.S. President William H. Taft opened Washington's 1910 season by tossing the ceremonial first pitch. Taft's opening pitch gave rise to the tradition of the chief executive tossing out the first pitch of the season. Taft was no Johnny-come-lately when it came to rooting for baseball. Having been an amateur player of some note around Cincinnati, Taft's first and favorite team was the legendary Red Stockings, who captured 88 consecutive victories in 1869. His interest continued through a cousin who owned the Chicago Cubs. Until George Bush visited several minor league games in progress, 1990-92, Taft was the only sitting president ever to visit a minor league game. His touring group drove on to the playing field at the Denver ballpark, October 3, 1911. This time he stayed for a shorter time than at the Washington game, which he left in the seventh inning. Taft was not the only president with more than a casual interest in the National Pastime.

Andrew Johnson was an honorary member of the New York Mutual Fire Hose Company. He encouraged the Mutuals to play in the ellipse behind the White House. He even stopped to watch a couple of innings at Swampdoodle Grounds on the way to his impeachment trial. Warren G. Harding owned a piece of the Marion, Ohio, franchise in the Ohio State League. Dwight D. Eisenhower played the outfield for Atchinson of the Kansas State League three months before he entered West Point and later between his junior and senior years at the Academy during a home visit to earn some spending money. Ike was also a star football player who was carried off the field during the famous Notre Dame-Army game when Gus Dorias and Knute Rockne proved the effectiveness of the forward pass. Richard M. Nixon attended more games as vice president than had any Washington executive since Postmaster General James Farley.

Performances

The First Old-timers Game
The Glory of their Times

1869

TOP: Players from the 1870s and 1880s participated in Boston's 1908 old-timers' game, playing under the rules they knew.
BOTTOM: Some of baseball's greatest living old-timers gathered for the Army-Navy Relief Fund in 1943. How many former stars can you name?

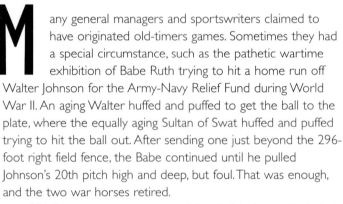

Many general managers and sportswriters claimed to have originated old-timers games. Sometimes they had a special circumstance, such as the pathetic wartime exhibition of Babe Ruth trying to hit a home run off Walter Johnson for the Army-Navy Relief Fund during World War II. An aging Walter huffed and puffed to get the ball to the plate, where the equally aging Sultan of Swat huffed and puffed trying to hit the ball out. After sending one just beyond the 296-foot right field fence, the Babe continued until he pulled Johnson's 20th pitch high and deep, but foul. That was enough, and the two war horses retired.

Old-timers games were never intended to be contests, but a chance to see a boyhood hero one more time. According to the *New England Base Ballist* the first "old-timers game" on record was played in September 1869, when a team comprised of the 1859 Excelsiors of Brooklyn (without star Jim Creighton, who died in 1862) played a match against the Excelsiors of 1869. Soon afterward, the Knickerbockers Base Ball Club played their younger men against their stalwarts of the past.

Another memorable exhibition took place September 24, 1908, when 43 professional and amateur Boston-area ballplayers from the 1870s and 1880s gathered to celebrate the National Pastime. The *Boston Transcript* labeled it "An Honest Old-time Game." Sixteen stars of Boston's professional glory days showed up, including Albert Spalding and Tommy Bond, Harry Shafer and Captain Billy Nash. The majority of the 27 college players were old Harvard men, but there were several from Yale, Dartmouth, M.I.T., Amherst and even the University of Iowa.

The men played under the rules they knew. They moved the pitcher's box 10 feet closer to the plate; the pitchers threw an underhand ball; and the batsmen called for a high or low ball. Batters had to have nine balls called before they took a base; they ran the danger of being out on caught foul tips; and the catchers could catch foul flies on the bounce and still have their man out. Also, to effect a double play, the catcher could drop the ball after a third strike, pick it up, touch home plate, and then nail the runner between bases, scoring a double play. A great time was had by all.

The First No-Hitter
and the First Perfect Game
Legacy of Perfection

1875
1880

J. Lee Richmond, who threw the first perfect game in 1880, had a cross-fire fastball that was tough on left-handed hitters. Baseball lost a great pitcher when Dr. Richmond left for the medical field.

oseph E. Borden was a small right-handed pitcher who lasted only parts of two seasons, yet catalogued two very important firsts. The son of a prominent New Jersey family, he played under the pseudonym of Nedrob (Borden backwards) and Joseph E. Josephs because his parents disapproved of his ballplaying activities.

On July 28, 1875, under the name Josephs he hurled the first and only no-hitter of the National Association, and of known baseball history. His 4-0 masterpiece for the Philadelphia club blanked the Chicago White Stockings. He won only one other game that year. His lack of success under the name Josephs did not stop him from signing a three-year contract with the Boston club in the new National League. On April 22, 1876, Boston and the Athletics played the very first National League game at the Athletics' home grounds at 25th and Jefferson streets in Philadelphia. A crowd of 3,000 saw Borden win 6-5 to become the first winning pitcher in National League history. Once again he failed to finish the season, but the thrifty Bostonians put Borden to work as the groundskeeper and ticket taker to work off his contract.

The first perfect game occurred in 1880. The game — with 27 men up and 27 men down and one batter thrown out at first by the right fielder — was hurled by J. Lee Richmond, who played baseball four years for Oberlin College, then studied medicine at Brown University. There he starred for the baseball team as a slugging outfielder and unhittable pitcher. During the 1879 season he pitched a no-hitter in an exhibition for the Worcesters of the minor league National Association against the Chicago White Stockings. He was signed immediately. One week later Brown won the college championship with Richmond in the points. (Prior to the mound and pitching rubber, four circular disks delineated the pitcher's area. The disks were called points.)

Richmond participated as both a professional and amateur player. Because of him the rules that prohibited pros from competing with amateurs were established. His pitching, which included a second professional no-hitter in 1879, so strengthened the Worcester club that it was invited to join the National League. There Richmond wasted no time in establishing himself as an extremely tough portsider. Platoon lefty versus righty match-ups began because of his sharp breaking curveball. Richmond — also the first medical doctor to play in the majors — was baseball's first left-handed ace. After his stupefying success, club officials began the illusive search for the portside pitching star.

As amazing as J. Lee Richmond's debut was another hurler's success a century later at the end of his lengthy career. Nolan Ryan came to the majors in 1966 and stayed 27 years, creating a no-hit legacy that may never be topped. Ryan struck out more batters and tossed more no-hitters that any man alive. He didn't just surpass the existing records, he shattered them. He left them so far behind that Lefty Carlton's 4,136 strikeouts and Sandy Koufax's four no-hit games were virtually forgotten by the younger crowd. In his career Ryan racked up 5,714 whiffs and seven no-hitters. He was still striking out 200-plus batters yearly at age 45.

The First Game in the National Association
Professional Players' League

1871

James "Deacon" White, here in an 1888 Detroit Wolverine uniform, led off in the first game of the first professional league in 1871. White and George Wright lived long enough to see the Baseball Hall of Fame established.

The first game of the new professional league was played at Fort Wayne on May 4, 1871, between the Cleveland Forest City club and the Fort Wayne Kekiongas. A full account of this "remarkable game," play by play, inning by inning, was printed in the Cleveland paper. From the account, the following excerpt has been selected.

"It was the finest game of baseball ever witnessed in the City, and the playing throughout was without precedent in the annals of base ball. The members of both clubs established without a doubt their reputations as among the most perfect base ball players in the United States. There was not an error by Cleveland and only three by Fort Wayne. The batting was not as heavy as in some games, although the pitching was superior, especially the pitching of Bobby Mathews. The Umpiring was fair, impartial and entirely satisfactory, to both clubs. Owing to the threatening indications of the weather, not over 500 persons were on the grounds. The enthusiasm ran high among the spectators and we doubt if a game in this country was ever witnessed with closer attention. The Kekiongas won the toss and sent Forest City to bat.

In the second inning, Lennon made a fine hit to left field and made second. Carey struck a fly to Allison who took it with one hand after a hard run, Lennon going to third. Mincher sent a fly to Kimball, then McDermott hit to first, bringing Lennon home. Kelly was out on a foul fly to Jim White.

Amid cheering and intense excitement, Fort Wayne made the second and last run of the game in the 5th inning. McDermott was out at first. Kelly hit past first, and went around to third on two passed balls. On Williams' out at first, Kelly tallied. Mathews was out on a foul bound to White."

Then came the rains in torrents and the game was called with Fort Wayne leading 2-0, leaving the Kekiongas without their ninth inning at the bat. Bobby Mathews was only 19 and pitched one of the four shutouts for the year. The fledgling league had gotten off to a rousing start.

The First Pitcher's Save
Fireman

1871
1969

In 1969 Bill Singer won 20 games for a Dodgers staff that boasted three future Hall of Fame pitchers: Don Drysdale, Don Sutton and Jim Bunning. That year Singer also posted baseball's first official save, on Opening Day.

The save became an official statistic in 1969. Chicago sportswriter Jerome Holtzman received credit for its establishment, though the concept had been around for quite some time.

On May 20, 1871, Harry Wright relieved Boston Red Stockings pitcher Al Spalding in the eighth inning of a National Association game versus the Philadelphia Athletics with the score 10-7 in favor of Boston, with one man on and one man out. Wright gave up a single and a scoring fly out, then retired the side with the Boston lead down to 10-8. The Red Stockings scored once in the top of the ninth, then Wright set the Athletics down in order in the bottom of the ninth to preserve an 11-8 victory. It was the first "save" in professional baseball.

The definition of the save changed through the years, but the result was always victory. The current save rule came into operation in 1975. It stated, "Credit a pitcher with a save when he meets all three of the following conditions: 1) he is the finishing pitcher in a game won by his club; and 2) he is not the winning pitcher; and 3) he qualifies under one of the following conditions: a) he enters the game with a lead of no more than three runs and pitches for at least one inning; or b) he enters the game with the potential tying run either on base, or at bat, or on deck; or c) he pitches effectively for at least three innings. No more than one save may be credited in each game." Older versions of the save were more limited. Usually the pitcher had to face the tying or winning run to qualify.

The first official save went to Bill Singer of the Los Angeles Dodgers. On Opening Day, April 7, 1969, he relieved Don Drysdale, who retired after six innings of four-hit ball with the score 3-2 in his favor. Singer blanked the hometown Cincinnati Reds on zero hits and one walk over the last three innings of the game. The lanky right-hander posted only two saves during his 14-year, 118-win career, but one of them was the very first as an official save statistic.

The First Pitcher to Win 1–0 With his own Home Run

Pud & Mac

1877

In 1877 James "Pud" Galvin no-hit the Red Stockings and homered for the only score. Galvin won 360 major league games and at least another 100 in the minors. A workhorse and prodigious eater, he sometimes weighed 300 pounds during the off-season.

How marvelous and how Ruthian it would be for a pitcher to win his own 1-0 game with a home run. It would be like Chip Hilton, Bronc Burnett, Frank Merriwell, Lefty Locke or the great Baseball Joe Matson winning their own games. But those were fictional characters. Has a real pitcher ever won his own game with a home run? Of course it has happened, but not very often.

On May 2, 1877, the Allegheny club (Pittsburgh) of the International Association upset the National League Boston Red Stockings in an exhibition game by a score of 1-0 when pitcher James "Pud" Galvin tossed a no-hitter and hit a home run for the contest's only score. And another unusual pitcher home run took place in 1879.

On July 26, 1879, Syracuse Star (National League) pitcher Harry McCormick hit a home run in the first inning and made it stand up through the entire game as he defeated Boston's hurler Tommy Bond by a score of 1-0. It was the first and only time in major league history that a pitcher won his own game with a first-inning home run.

The First Shutout
Goose Eggs

1870

BELOW: Bob Gibson presents his glove to Ken Smith, director of the Baseball Hall of Fame, the day after he fanned 17 Detroit Tigers in Game One of the 1968 World Series. He posted 13 shutouts during the regular season.

BOTTOM: Christy Mathewson once tossed a 14-hit shutout. He gave up two hits in each of the first seven frames, then tightened up to retire the last six batters in order. The Hall of Famer threw three shutouts in the 1905 World Series.

The verb shut out meant a baseball pitcher limited the opposition to zero runs. The term was borrowed from horseracing, where it meant a bettor who failed to get his bet down before the window closed. He was shut out of betting. Other terms which meant the same thing were calcimined, whitewashed and Chicagoed.

The latter word was coined on July 23, 1870, when Rynie Wolters of the New York Mutuals shut out the Chicago White Stockings by a score of 9 to 0. Shutouts prior to that date had been few and far between: only five shutout games had ever been played and they were all between amateur clubs. This was the first professional shutout and it was tossed in the following fashion.

Six thousand fans crowded into the renovated Chicago ballgrounds. The old one had been burned to a crisp in the Great Chicago Fire. The system of seats and comfortable stands provided reporters and fans alike with a great view of the action on the immaculately groomed playing field. The crowd saw "the finest fielding game ever played." But at bat the Chicago boys were too anxious. Mutual pitcher Wolters took advantage of this and gave them nothing good to hit. Chicago managed only two hits off Wolters' hurling. The New York papers wasted no time in chortling and harassing Chicago. They explained that they no longer would use "skunked, or whitewashed or goose-egged, but Chicagoed." The term survived into the 1920s.

Other remarkable shutout performances included Christy Mathewson tossing three shutouts in the 1905 World Series. Grover C. Alexander tossed 16 whitewashings in tiny Baker Bowl during the 1916 season. Years later Bob Gibson completed 28 of 34 starts with 13 shutouts and a 1.12 ERA during the 1968 season. His 22-9 record perplexed historians as to how he could have lost nine times.

The First Pitcher to Strike Out 20 in a Game
Two-time Offender

1986

Baseball hasn't played well at the movies because real life has been so much more unpredictable than Hollywood. Buck O'Neil, the octogenarian spokesman for the Negro Leagues, said, "Fans looked at Bo Jackson because they wanted to see something they had never seen." Followers of Roger Clemens also saw the impossible, twice.

On April 29, 1986, a cold day at Fenway Park, Clemens set down 20 Seattle Mariners on strikes. The feat inspired the 23-year-old Texan to wins in 14 of his first 15 starts. He was the runaway choice for the Cy Young Award that year. Ten years later, the Texas Thunderbolt struck again.

This time Roger Clemens salvaged a poor year and failing contract talks with a five-hit, 20-strikeout, zero-walk performance on September 18, 1996, versus the Detroit Tigers. This time the Special K show took place on the road. The game failed to impress those who held the Boston purse strings, and the 34-year-old Texan took his show to Toronto, where he won another Cy Young Award in 1997.

Another pitching first occurred in 1998, when the Cubs' rookie pitcher Kerry Wood astonished the baseball world by whiffing 20 in one game — no freshman feat.

The First All-Star Game
Showtime!

1933

TOP: Lou Gehrig and batboy Johnny McBride greet Babe Ruth following his two-run homer in the third inning of the very first All-Star Game in 1933.
BOTTOM: The 1933 NL All-Star team wore special uniforms for the occasion, as did their AL counterparts.

The earliest pure all-star contest on record would be the 1858 Fashion Race Course series on Long Island, when the stars from New York challenged the best of Brooklyn. The contests "excited the greatest enthusiasm and spirit among the lovers of the sport at that period." New York won the first game 22-18 amid very little betting, an anomaly for the time, but respective of what a close game the contest really was. The second was captured by Brooklyn 29-8 with considerable money changing hands. New York backers were greatly influenced by the outcome of the first contest. The rubber match was captured by New York over the heavily-favored Brooklyn boys.

The first All-Star Game as we know it — American League versus National League — took place as an exhibition at Comiskey Park in 1933. In true Ruthian fashion, the Babe belted a two-run homer in the third inning that made the difference in the American League's 4-2 victory. That contest would demonstrate superiority of one league over the other. The first All-Star Game was the creation of Arch Ward of Chicago. He patterned the game out of the holiday basketball tournaments held in New York and Chicago. The idea of a Game of Stars was to be a one-year, one-shot deal. The players and managers — Connie Mack, and from retirement, John McGraw — liked the event so much that it was continued.

In the early years the American League, led by Yankee players and Boston's Ted Williams, dominated the National League 12 wins to 4, then in 1950 Red Schoendienst walloped a home run in the 14th inning to lead the Nationals over the Americans. After seesawing back and forth during the fifties, the Senior Circuit showed its power. Led by Willie Mays, Stan Musial, Pete Rose and others, the Nationals won 23, lost 2 and tied 1 from 1960 until 1983. The Nationals' pluck played out in 1988, when American League domination returned. This time it was led by the likes of Cal Ripken, Ruben Sierra, Wade Boggs, Frank Thomas and Ken Griffey, Jr.

The First Hall of Fame Game
First Ups!

1939

Honus Wagner (left) and
Eddie Collins, captains for
the NL and AL respectively,
chose first ups the old-
fashioned way at the first
annual Hall of Fame game,
June 12, 1939.

The 1939 Hall of Fame dedication ceremonies in Cooperstown thrilled everyone who participated. And the stars really showed up. They came by train to the quaint village in upstate New York. Every living Hall of Fame member attended. The big leaguers marched down Main Street, where they were joined by an array of boys and girls dressed in 1839 costumes. It was a colorful escort for the Hall of Famers.

The procession swung into Doubleday Field, where some 8,000 spectators filled the picturesque ballpark to capacity. The festivities opened with a game of "Town Ball," performed by players in period costume. The game was supervised by a gentleman in stovepipe hat, long, tight trousers and flowered waistcoat. Mustached soldiers appeared next and re-enacted a game of the 1850s between the Excelsiors and the Knickerbockers. Geraldine Farrar, the operatic star, reminded the audience that her father had once played first base for Philadelphia. Lieutenant Daniel C. Doubleday, West Point 1929, a descendant of the game's mythical founder, was presented and spoke on behalf of his pioneering ancestor.

Walter Johnson batted grounders for the all-star practice. American and National Leaguers mixed for a picnic-style game, and then Eddie Collins and Honus Wagner chose for first at-bats by gripping hand-over-hand up the bat handle. The game itself was fun as the players were there to be seen and have fun. Line-up changes were frequent. The Wagners won 4-2 in seven innings as the game was called to enable the baseball people to catch special trains to all points of the country.

The First Sunday Game in the National League

A New Tradition

1892

Billy Sunday, a light-hitting speed merchant, quit baseball after the Players' League debacle to enter into evangelicalism full time. His rousing sermons included such baseball metaphors as sliding at the home plate of God and knocking the Devil out of the box.

No other issue so dominated baseball in the nineteenth and early twentieth centuries as baseball on Sunday. Players were hauled before local magistrates. Clubs loaded their players onto special trains to suburbs where baseball on the Christian Sabbath was legal. Cincinnati was expelled from the National League for refusing to sign an agreement which prohibited Sunday ball. During the 1880s the American Association rivaled the National League on the strengths of Sunday ball, free flowing beer, and 25-cent admission. The AA cities did make concessions to the huge, well-dressed, Sunday crowds by offering sections of no alcohol and no smoking.

When the old AA broke up and four teams came into the National League (1892), the provisions were Sunday baseball where legal plus optional 25-cent admission. Opposition that had been so steadfast in the 1880s melted in the wake of 18,000-plus crowds on Sundays. Schedule maker and league president Nick Young could not accommodate all the clubs who wanted lucrative Sunday dates in the western cities. By the turn of the century, only Philadelphia, Boston and New York still had laws that prohibited Sunday play.

To prove how reluctant some in baseball were to turn from the past, the Texas Rangers played the first Sunday night game in 1973, 38 years after night baseball became part of the major league scene. Sunday baseball had the commercial effect of drawing more than all of the weekday games put together. The time slot became so important that teams played doubleheaders to accomodate working men who would bring their children to games. Sunday pitchers such as Ted Lyons or Freddie Fitzsimmons hurled one game per week. The day was truly sacred for an audience that worked six days per week.

ABOVE: The first major league night game, in Cincinnati on May 24, 1935, drew a capacity crowd. The second caused a near riot in which Kitty Burke, a night-club singer, batted and Cardinal manager Frank Frisch was ejected for arguing that her out counted.

RIGHT: Commissioner Bowie Kuhn suggested that some World Series games could be played at night.

BASEBALL
OFFICE OF THE
COMMISSIONER

The First Game Played at Night

Jose, Can you See?

1880
1935

Bruce Kison (right), winner of the first World Series night game in 1971, gets ready to board a helicopter with best man Bob Moose in order to make Kison's wedding that night, after the Pirates won Game Seven in Baltimore, 2–1.

T he first baseball game under artificial lights was played in Hull, Massachusetts, between teams representing rival department stores, on September 2, 1880. The Whites beat the Reds 14 to 13 in a dimly lit contest. Play was fine around the plate and infield, but next to impossible in the outfield. Then, on July 7, 1909, Grand Rapids and Zanesville of the Central League played seven innings after sundown in artificial light. But these were exhibitions.

Des Moines of the Western League announced that it would open the 1930 season under lights. The notice set off a frenzy of activity among clubs wanting to be the first to play under the artificial arcs. On April 28, 1930, night baseball became a reality as Independence (Kansas) of the Western Association staged the inaugural night game of Organized Ball. On the same date, the Kansas City Monarchs of the Negro Leagues played a game using portable lights in Enid, Oklahoma. Finally, Des Moines played their announced home night game.

Night baseball at the major league level was proposed by Cincinnati General Manager Larry MacPhail. It had been successful in the minors, Negro Leagues and on the barnstorming circuits. Reluctant at first, the National League granted Cincinnati only seven night games, the first being on May 24, 1935. They were so successful that the National League soon heartily endorsed the lit matches.

The World Series stubbornly clung to day games despite the heavy night-time schedules in both leagues. The first night game in the Fall Classic was Game Four of the 1971 Series between Pittsburgh and Baltimore. Pittsburgh's rookie Bruce Kison replaced a shell-shocked Luke Walker with six innings of one-hit relief to knot the Series at 2-2. When Commissioner Bowie Kuhn saw that 61 million TV viewers had watched the game, he ordered all weekday games to be played at night.

The First Modern World Series

A Test of the Best

1903

The World Series of 1903 generated fanatical crowd support outside of Huntington Avenue Grounds in Boston. The Fall Classic still inspires loyal enthusiasm.

Pirates owner Barney Dreyfus had just engineered the 1903 peace agreement between warring factions of the National and American Leagues when he received a challenge from the Boston Americans. The series of championship games was accepted by Dreyfus without conferring with his manager Fred Clarke. Had he done so, he would had known that the Pirates had only one serviceable pitcher, Deacon Phillippe. Dreyfus unknowingly consigned his team to certain failure for the sake of peace between the rival major leagues.

Boston, led by Hall of Fame hurlers Cy Young and Big Bill Dinneen, defeated Pittsburgh in the best-of-nine series by winning the last four games, including two from the tiring Phillippe, who won three and lost two with five complete games for the Series. The World Series was a smashing success with both fans and players.

Still smarting from the National League defeat in that World Series, Giants owner John T. Brush refused to play the 1904 American League Champions. He then made suggestions to the National Commission to govern play between the American and National League winners. These suggestions, once approved, became the Brush Rules and are still in effect today. They provide for a seven-game series, a 60-40 percent split of the receipts from the first four games, with 5 percent going to each league. Receipts from subsequent Series games were split evenly between the two clubs. Fortunately for Brush, the Giants won the 1905 Series. As in 1904, the World Series remained the ultimate bargaining chip among baseball executives.

AMHERST EXPRESS.

EXTRA.

WILLIAMS AND AMHERST
BASE BALL AND CHESS!
MUSCLE AND MIND!!

July 1st and 2d, 1859.

THE ORIGIN OF THE MATCH.

At the commencement of this term, it was privately proposed among the Amherst students to challenge Williams College to a game of Ball. In the second or third week the challenge was given by the committee of the College. Notice had been privately sent to Williams of this intention, that both parties might have equal opportunity of practice. The challenge was readily accepted, and in turn Williams challenged to a game at Chess, that there might be "a trial of mind as well as muscle." This being at once agreed upon, the agents of the two colleges met at Chester Factories on the 8th of June, to discuss and settle preliminaries. Some difficulties were found, Williams declining to play, except at Pittsfield. As the challenge provided that the match should be played "at some intermediate place," the Amherst agent thought it should be understood as fairly and equally intermediate, and insisted on this. Several places were spoken of, but the agents separated without any positive agreement. At this time, the Base-Ball Club of Pittsfield offered, by their President Mr. Plunkett, their grounds for the match ; and the Chess Club, by Mr. Davis, their rooms. These courteous offers decided the question of a meeting of the colleges, and were accepted with thanks. The 1st of July was chosen for the game of Ball, the following day for the Chess. The rules of Ball were, in substance, those of the Massachusetts Association recently adopted. The number of players was fixed at thirteen ; the number of tallies on the score at sixty-five. The rules adopted in Chess were those of the New York Club.

state this, to correct reports to the contrary. Williams appeared in the uniform of club belts, Amherst decidedly in undress. In size and muscular development, we thought Amherst, on the whole, superior ; while in agility, in running and leaping, the Williams boys excelled. By some ridiculous mistake a report was spread that the thrower from Amherst was the professional blacksmith of the place, hired for the occasion This rumor afforded great amusement to that very fine player, and his comrades. A bystander remarked that the story seemed probable, for nobody but a blacksmith could throw in such a manner, for three hours and a half. Each party furnished its own ball for throwing. The Amherst ball weighed 2¼ oz., and was 6¼ inches around. It was made by Mr. Henry Hebard of North Brookfield, Mass., and was really a work of art. The Williams ball, we judged to be 7 inches in circumference, and not to exceed in weight 2 oz. It was also covered with leather of some light color, drab or buff, so as not to be easily distinguished by the batter.

THE GROUNDS. THE DAY.

A field had been hired for the occasion, north of the "Town lot," and east of the Maplewood Institute ; the ground lay smooth, and was well adapted to the long front-and-back play of the Massachusetts game. The weather was glorious. Either party might have taken the omen of Austerlitz from the magnificent rising of the sun of that day. It rose for Amherst.

THE SPECTATORS.

A large and excited company of ladies and gentlemen from the place watched the whole

A. J. Quick, S. W. Pratt, J. H. Knox, J. E. Bush, R. E. Beecher, H. F. C. Nichols, (umpire, C. R. Taft.)

Referee.—W. R. Plunkett, Esq., President of the Pittsfield Base Ball Club.

SYNOPSIS OF THE GAME.

Amherst held the first inning by lot, and Williams played the last by turn. Williams played best at first, making ten tallies to Amherst's one ; when the latter went in to win, and made twenty to their one, and kept the advantage throughout, making more than two tallies for one.

THE GAME BY INNINGS.

1st Amherst opened : Claflin—home run, back strike, Tower caught out by Bush, (W) Parker put out on 4th base by Storrs—Amherst, 1 tally.

2d. Evans caught out by Pratt, (W) Parker caught out by Tower—A. 1 tally, W. 9.

3d. Cushman caught out by Pratt, (W), Fitch caught out by Claflin—A. 8, W. 0.

4th. Evans caught out by Pratt, (W) Blagden put out by Cushman, 2d base—tallies 0.

5th. Roome ticked out, caught by Pratt, (W) Pratt the same by Claflin—A. 12, W. 1.

RECESS.

6th. Gridley caught out by Hastings, longfield, (W) Anderson caught out by Claflin—A. 0, W. 2.

7th. Roome caught out by Anderson, (W) Fitch by Claflin, several fine knocks from Amherst, Amherst leads 29—12.

8th. Gridley caught out by Bush, (W) Blagden hit at 1st base by Claflin—tallies 0.

9th. Pratt hit on 1st base by Anderson, (W) Hastings caught out by Evans—tallies 0.

considerable delay on a reference to the umpires, Storrs made a home knock, on the front field, fine run for Amherst, making 12 tallies, W. 0.

17th. Gridley caught out by Simmons, (W) Quick caught out by Hyde—tallies 0.

18th. Tomson out on 3d base, (W) Beecher caught out by Claflin, each makes 1 tally.

19th. Storrs out by Fitch, (good catch,) (W) Parker caught out by Claflin—tallies 0.

20th. Cushman caught out by Simmons, (W) Fitch hit by Evans on 4th base—tal 0.

21st. Hyde hit by Fitch on 3d base, (W) Brown hit on 4th base by Storrs. Each makes 3 tallies.

22d. Pierce caught out by Quick (W) Beecher put out by Cushman on 2d base—A. 4, W. 1.

23d. Evans put out by Blagden 2d base, (W) Fitch put out at 1st base by Hyde—A. 2, W. 1.

24th. Pratt ticked out, caught by Anderson, (W) Blagden caught out by Claflin—A. 2, W. 1. Amherst boys within two tallies of winning, the strife was then to determine whether they should make two for one which seemed not unlikely.

25th. Tomson caught out by Anderson, (W) Bush caught out by Gridley—Williams 3 tallies.

26th. Gridley ticked out, caught by Anderson, (W) out by player unknown. The last inning The Amherst boys ran around, entirely regardless of danger or appearances. They made their bases as if they were thinking of 75 tallies, which was the number proposed by them for the game. However they

---

The First College Baseball Game
Amherst vs. Williams

1859

This account presented a play-by-play of baseball's first college game, between Amherst and Williams colleges in 1859.

On July 1, 1859, students from Amherst and Williams colleges in Massachusetts gathered on the common at Pittsfield, Massachusetts, to play the first intercollegiate baseball match. The match was played under 1857 rules for the Massachusetts game, although some slight modifications were made to suit the convenience of the two teams. Amherst won the contest by a score of 73 to 32. A local report mentioned that "Williams appeared in the uniform of club boys, Amherst decidedly in undress. In size and muscular development, Amherst on the whole superior; while in agility, in running and leaping the Williams boys excelled."

The contest was just one part of the challenge. The second was a chess match. This meeting of the minds was also won by Amherst, which gave cause for great rejoicing when the brawn and brain returned to campus. The bells rang and bands of students paraded throughout the town until sunrise the next morning.

One hundred years later the schools of Amherst and Williams commemorated the first college game with another game played under the same rules.

The First Playing of "The Star Spangled Banner"

It Happened in Brooklyn

1862

An Oakland neighborhood choir sings "The Star Spangled Banner" before a game at the Oakland Coliseum, carrying on a baseball tradition that began in 1862.

Katie Casey was baseball mad,
Had the fever and had it bad;
Just to root for the hometown crew,
Ev'ry sou, Katie blew.
On a Saturday, her young beau,
Called to see if she'd like to go,
To see a show but Miss Kate said, "No,
I'll tell you what you can do"
Take me out to the ball game,
Take me out to the crowd,
Buy me some peanuts and cracker jack,
I don't care if I never get back,
Let me root, root, root, for the home team,
If they don't win it's a shame.
For it's one, two, three strikes, you're out,
At the old ball game.

William Cammeyer enclosed Union Grounds in Brooklyn. When the grounds were opened on May 15, 1862, a band was on hand to celebrate the event. It began patriotically with "The Star Spangled Banner," and marked the first time there was music at a ball game. The tune did not become the national anthem until Herbert Hoover signed it into law many years later. The song was not played exclusively in baseball until World War II, when patriotic fervor demanded it for every game. Other songs that were played at the start of ball games included "Columbia, the Gem of the Ocean." There was also another song closely associated with baseball.

It was a song written by two men who had never seen a major league game nor had any interest in the sport. "Take Me Out to the Ball Game" was the work of Jack Norworth and Albert von Tilzer, two successful music professionals. Norworth wrote the lyrics for the song during a half-hour New York City subway ride, getting the idea from an 1908 advertisement that suggested customers take in a baseball game at the Polo Grounds.

Tilzer and Norworth figured they'd bombed when the song was first introduced at the Amphion Theatre in Brooklyn. Three months later at the famed Hammerstein's Victoria Theater, he was surprised to find that several performers before him had incorporated "Take Me Out to the Ball Game" in their acts. A hit was born. It was one of four baseball songs to come out in 1908. Only the chorus became popular; not one fan in a stadium could sing the whole song, which appears on the left.

The First Batter to Lay Down a Bunt

Baby Hits

1866

Leadoff batter for the old Baltimore Orioles, Willie Keeler used the bunt effectively to help him post a .343 career batting average.

Throughout baseball history the bunt or "baby hit" was the great equalizer. It sought to take advantage of a hole in the defense. It was the pure essence of baseball, taking advantage of the opposition.

Nobody knew what Tom Barlow of the Brooklyn Atlantics was thinking in 1866 when he laid down a purposefully puny hit, then beat the throw to first. Undoubtedly the surprised infielder held the ball as if to say "what is this?" Answer: the first bunt.

The disdain that nineteenth-century hitters held for bunters did not prevent Barlow and Dickey Pearce from becoming proficient at the art. The old Baltimore Orioles — legendary because they won three straight pennants in the 12-team National League — were quite adept at pushing the ball to all corners of the infield. Their leadoff batter, Willie Keeler, used the bunt and peculiar nineteenth-century strike rules to post the 13th highest career batting average of all time (.343).

Foul balls did not count as strikes until 1901. Bunt fouls were rung up as strikes in 1894, though it was 1902 before a batter was called out after failing to bunt safely on the third strike. A hot National League strategy during the 1890s was to drag bunt for base hits. If he laid it down fair the bunter had a good chance of beating it out. If the baby hit rolled foul he could try it again. League moundsmen were besieged by third-strike bunters. The burly Cy Young employed his own strategy for ridding the game of the bunt nuisance.

On a foul bunt attempt, Young would meet the batter coming back from first base and explain to him that he only got two foul balls each at-bat. The next pitch, explained Cy, would be right between the eyes. Early in his career Young didn't suffer the fatigue from chasing bunts that other pitchers did. But eventually it caught up with him, as covering the bunt forced the end to his career (after 511 wins) and to fellow Hall of Famer Walter Johnson's 417-win career.

The First Batter to Hit a Home Run in his First Big League At-bat

Big Bang Debut

1887

RIGHT: Cleveland's Earl Averill came to major league baseball after a stellar season in the Pacific Coast League. He hit a home run in his first at-bat in 1929.

BOTTOM: New York's pitcher Hoyt Wilhelm homered in his big league debut for the only round-tripper of his 20-year career.

Millions of Little Leaguers dream of hitting a home run on their first at-bat in the majors. Dozens of players have done so. Only two Hall of Fame members, Earl Averill and Hoyt Wilhelm, ripped home runs in their initial at-bats. In Wilhelm's career he won the National League ERA title in 1954, but never hit another roundtripper in a career that lasted from 1952 to 1972.

Other notable first time smackers included bespectacled Bob Nieman who whacked homers in his first two at-bats with the St. Louis Cardinals in 1951, and went on to smash 125 four-base blows in his career. Earl Averill, who smacked his debut home run in 1929, picked up 238 dingers, the most by a player who homered in his big league debut until Gary Gaetti smashed his record with 332 home runs through the 1997 season.

To find the first batter who homered in his debut, look to the old American Association. On Opening Day, April 16, 1887, Mike Griffin with Baltimore (lifetime 42 homers) and George "Whitewings" Tebeau from Cincinnati both stroked clean four-base hits in their first major league at-bats. Griffin played 11 more years and Tebeau became a well-known club owner and ballpark builder in Denver and Kansas City.

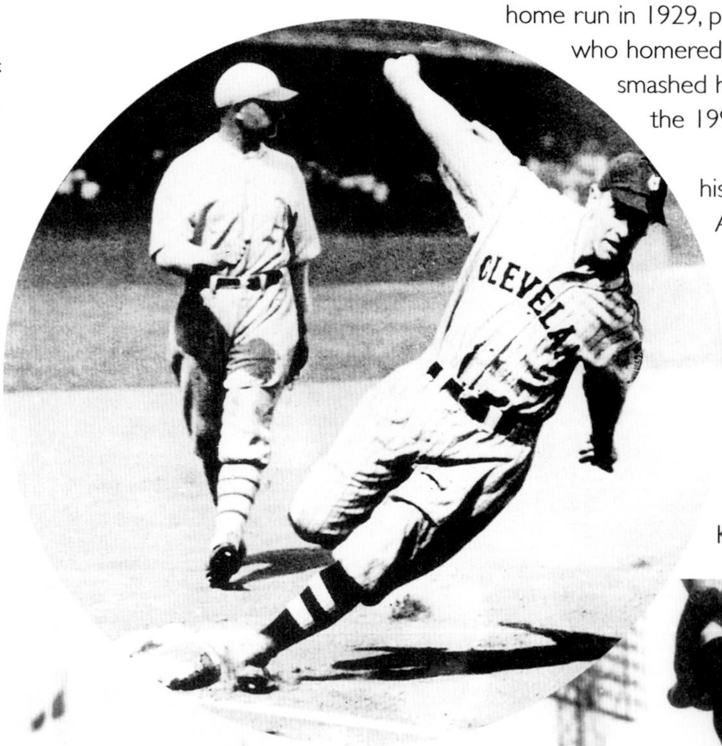

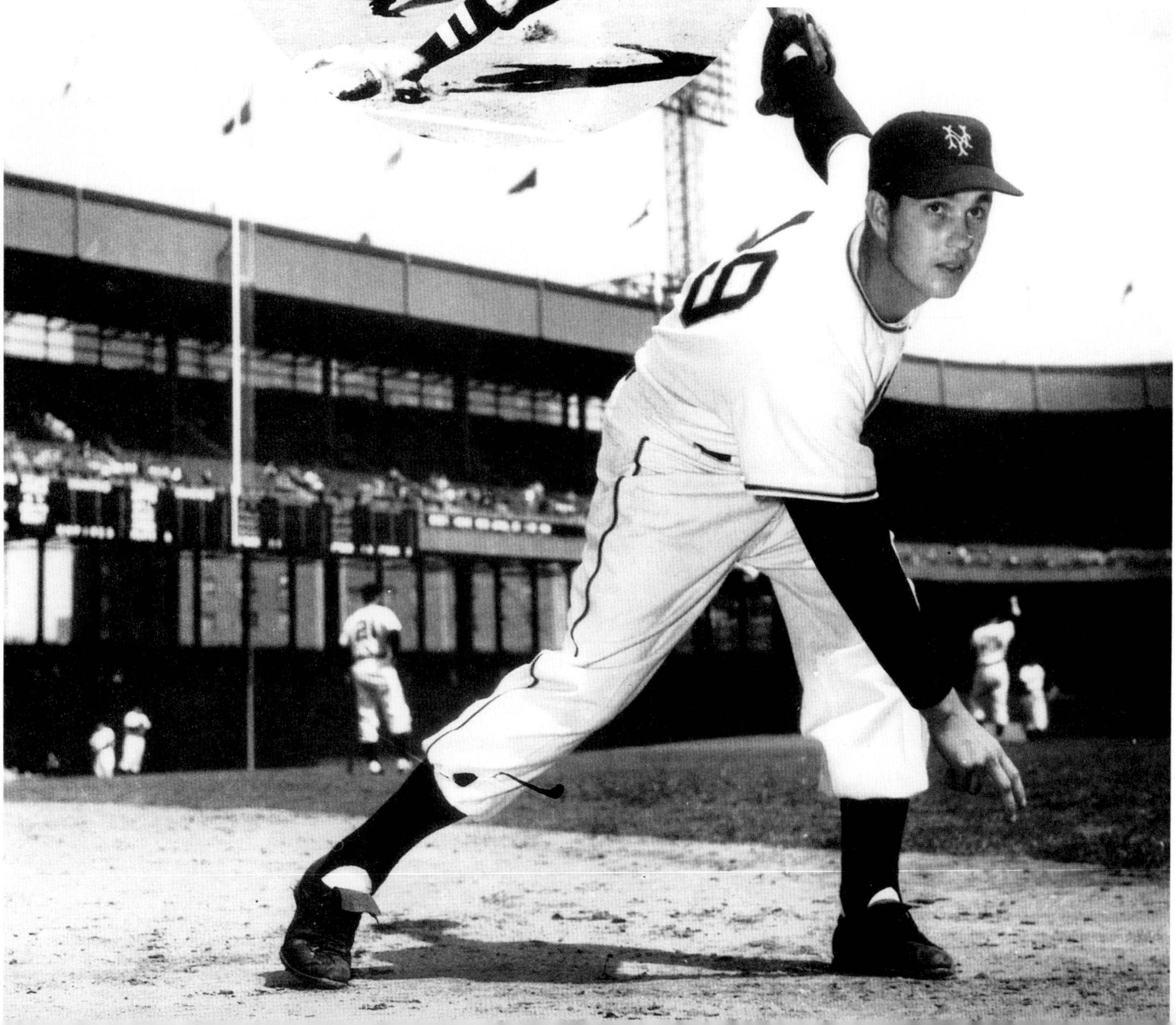

The First Unassisted Triple Play
Three for One

1878

TOP LEFT: Cleveland
second baseman Bill
Wambsganss.
TOP RIGHT: Wambsganss
turned a triple play in the
1920 World Series.
BOTTOM: Shortstop Neal
Ball (center) with Amby
McConnell and Heinie
Wagner.

The first unassisted triple killing fostered a controversy. The facts were undisputed. In a 1878 National League contest, Boston's Jim O'Rourke drew a base on balls and scored when Providence's second baseman Charles Sweasy threw Jack Manning's drive over first sacker Tim Murnane's head, Manning going to third on the error. Murnane muffed Ezra Sutton's fly, and Manning held third as Sutton took second. Jack Burdock, the next batter, dropped a fly ball just over shortstop Tom Carey's head for what looked like a safe hit. Manning and Sutton proceeded to the home plate, meaning both runners crossed third base. Paul Hines ran in and caught the ball, and kept going to tag third. Outfielder Hines then tossed the ball to second, but it was unnecessary as both runners were out at third.

According to the rules of the day, and today, a runner must retouch the bases in order when tagging up. Thus, when Hines touched third, both runners were out! Every half century the description of the play surfaced and the researcher thought that he had discovered a mistake in baseball history, but the throw to Sweasy was unnecessary as the third out had already been made.

Shortstop Neal Ball of Cleveland turned the first triple killing of the twentieth century on July 19, 1909. Heine Wagner of Boston was on second base and Jake Stahl was on first base. Both of the men started with a rush in a hit-and-run play, when Ambrose McConnell rapped a line drive straight into Ball's hands. Ball ran over to second base and touched it before Wagner could get back, then ran toward Stahl and touched him out before he could return to first base, thereby making the triple play complete. He made the play in the second inning, the same inning in which he swatted a home run. It was the first unassisted triple play in the American League. Others have turned the trick as well, including a World Series spin.

Bill Wambsganss of Cleveland performed the feat in the 1920 World Series against the Brooklyn Dodgers. Six shortstops (Neal Ball, Ernie Padgett of the Boston Braves, Pittsburgh's Glenn Wright, the Cubs' Jim Cooney, Washington's Ron Hanson and Red Sox John Valentin) have turned the trick. Two second basemen (Wambganss and the Phillies' Mickey Morandini) and two first sackers (George Burns of the Red Sox and the Tigers' Johnny Neun) conclude the major league list.

The First Batter to Hit Four Home Runs in One Game

Bats on Fire

 1894

BOTTOM LEFT: Bobby Lowe hit only 17 home runs in 1894, but four of them came in one game for a historic first.
BOTTOM RIGHT: Mike Schmidt belted four homers in an 18–16 slugfest at Wrigley Field in 1976.

Of the 13 players who have four homers in one game, two came during baseball's dead ball era when the ball center was made of India rubber instead of cork. The first, Bobby Lowe, took advantage of the most spectacular ballpark fire since the Great Chicago Fire of 1871 when Boston's South End Grounds erupted into flames while members of the 1894 Baltimore Orioles and Boston Beaneaters were engaged in a fist fight at third base. The amazed ballplayers watched the hungry flames lick the top of the right field fence and shoot toward the grandstand. The players stopped their feud to help evacuate the stands. Not one spectator was seriously hurt, though the fire devastated a six-block area of Boston. The ball team had to move their next scheduled games to the old Congress Street Grounds where the Players' League had played and where the left field fence was only 250 feet from home plate.

Bobby Lowe was batting leadoff for the Boston Beaneaters when he connected on four line drives that sailed "far over the fence." It was the second game of the annual Decoration Day (Memorial) doubleheader. Lowe had gone 0 for 6 in the opener. After making an out to lead off the second contest, Lowe opened the third inning with a shot to left, over the fence. Later in the same inning he homered again, this time with a man on. He had a solo home run in the fifth, a three-run homer in the sixth and a single in the eighth. The four straight home run knocks were not duplicated until Lou Gehrig chose the day that John McGraw retired in 1932 to blast four consecutive home runs.

Of the other four-time home run hitters, Big Ed Delehanty of the Phillies deserves mention for his four homers and a single on July 13, 1896, which tied Lowe's single-game record of 17 total bases. Bob Horner, who never played in the minors, smacked his four homers on nationwide television in 1986 in a losing effort. Another Phillie, Mike Schmidt, smacked four, including the game-winner in the 10th inning of an 18-16 slugfest at Wrigley Field in 1976. The last slugger with four four-baggers was the little known Mark Whiten who, trying to make the club in St. Louis after less than spectacular seasons with Toronto, performed brilliantly for one night — September 7, 1993 — when he clubbed four homers and drove in 12 runs, tying Jim Bottomley's single-game RBI record.

The First Batter Caught with a Corked Bat
Magic Wands

1974

The baseball rule stated that "no bat may be made of pieces of wood glued together." Therefore, drilling a hole in the end of a bat, stuffing it with superballs, cork or Styrofoam, and resealing it with a wooden plug, was illegal.

Cap Anson of the Chicago ball club was caught by newspaper reporters using a bat made of several separate pieces of ash, glued together lengthwise. Through the center, Anson inserted a rattan rod about one-inch square, and composed of 12 strips of rattan firmly glued together, running from end to end of the bat. The handle was wound with linen cord. Anson was caught but not punished in 1884.

Norm Cash of the Tigers was another who was caught later, but not punished. He used a "special" stick in 1961 when he smashed 41 homers, scored 119 runs, batted in 132 and walked 124 times. His .361 batting average and .488 on-base percentage that year were career marks. Cash never again challenged the levels of his 1961 season. Years later, Cash admitted that he was aided by a corked bat. Seldom did a player get caught red-handed with the stuffed bat, but it happened.

Graig Nettles of the Yankees singled during the fifth inning of doubleheader on September 8, 1974. As the hit rocketed into left, the fat end of the bat fell off at the feet of Tiger catcher Bill Freehan, who was no stranger to loaded bats, having played with Cash and watched him pump in the cork. Freehan showed the offending bat to plate umpire Lou DiMuro, who negated the hit and removed the bat, which Nettles claimed a Yankee fan in Chicago gave to him for "good luck." The Tigers wanted the second inning home run by Nettles, which was the only run in the game, negated also. This the umpire could not do. According to baseball rules all protests must be made immediately. Once the next pitch occurs, all play stands as performed. Nettles faced a suspension for this fiasco.

In a 1987 game, Houston outfielder Billy Hatcher swung, making contact with the ball but splitting his bat. Several inches of cork flew out. Hatcher claimed, "I had no idea the bat was corked." He was ejected and suspended for 10 days. Hatcher and Nettles were the only batters ever suspended for corking despite Cash's admission and Amos Otis's claim of using superballs. The fact that players have tried to cheat proved that baseball was, and is, truly a little boy's game played by slightly more mature men.

The First Intentional Walk
Free Pass

1886

BELOW: Tip O'Neill, who took baseball's first intentional walk, won the AA Triple Crown in 1887.
BELOW RIGHT: Barry Bonds was intentionally passed with the bases loaded in 1998.

Several years ago members of the Society for American Baseball Research tried to find the first intentional walk. They found that twice enemy batsmen had been passed intentionally with the bases loaded: Nap Lajoie (Philadelphia Athletics) on May 23, 1901, and Swish Nicholson (Chicago Cubs) on July 23, 1944. In 1998 it happened again, when the Cardinals walked Barry Bonds with the bases loaded.

The earliest intentional pass came in Game Four of the 1886 World Championships between the St. Louis Browns and Chicago White Stockings in a winner-take-all series. It was the only championship series ever played under such cut-throat rules. Chicago was leading the Series two games to one, and the game 3-2.

In an eyewitness account, with one out St. Louis' Doc Bushong took his base on balls, then went to second on Arlie Latham's safe hit to third. Each advanced a base on Bob Caruthers' out, leaving first base open. Tip O'Neill then took first on balls *deliberately* pitched by John Clarkson. Next Bill Gleason came to bat and hit a grounder to center, which brought Bushong and Latham home. Charlie Comiskey hit safely to center, scoring O'Neill and sending Gleason to third. Curt Welch fouled out to end the historic inning.

The *New York Times* reported another intentional pass in a 1899 game. Philadelphia's Ed Delehanty, the visitors' left fielder, arranged a play that stopped the locals from taking the lead in the eighth inning. The Giants' John Warner was at third base and Kid Gleason on second with only one out. Jack Fifield, the visitors' pitcher, was none too steady. Tom O'Brien went up to bat. He was hitting Fifield's curves in the previous innings. Delehanty saw disaster if O'Brien got a hit. He ran up to Fifield and told him to give O'Brien a base on balls. This was done, and the piece of strategy worked exactly as Delehanty had figured. Fred Hartman hit a grounder to Monte Cross, who retired O'Brien at second base and Hartman at first on a double play.

The intentional pass became an official statistic in 1955. The all-time leader is Willie McCovey, but Barry Bonds has led the big leagues in securing intentional passes multiple times in the 1990s. He was purposefully passed 32 times in 1992 and 34 in 1997.

The First Hit-and-Run Play
A Scientific Strategy

Mike "King" Kelly played on nine pennant winners in 16 years, and helped initiate the hit-and-run as an offensive tool in Chicago in the 1880s. His sale by the Chicago White Stockings to the Boston Red Stockings for $10,000 forever changed the way club owners looked at their players.

John Montgomery Ward described the hit-and-run play, without naming it, in his book *Base Ball: How to Become a Player*. When the book was published in 1888, the play was already a standard offensive ploy known as "playing for the side." This phrase meant teamwork in moving runners around, as opposed to swinging for long hits. One of the reasons advanced in opposition to heavy hitting was all of the energy spent running the bases for only one run. Ward classified batters into two categories: those who swing at the ball and those who push at the ball. Cap Anson and King Kelly of the White Stockings were among those who pushed the ball. Bat control was essential to executing the hit-and-run play perfectly.

Ward explained, "the advantage of this (place hitting) to the player himself and to his team cannot be overestimated. For example, there is a runner on first who signals to the batter that he will try to steal second on the second ball pitched. When he starts to run the second baseman goes for his base and the entire field between first and second is left open. Now, if the batter gets a ball anywhere within reach and taps it down toward right field, the chances are that it will be safe, and the runner from first will keep right on to third. Often times, too, the batter himself will reach second on the throw from right field to third to catch the runner ahead of him. Now, by a little head-work, are runners on third and second, whereas, an attempt to smash the ball, trusting to luck as to where it should go, might have resulted in a double play or at least one man out and no advantage gained. Many a game is won by such scientific work."

The 1880s Chicago White Stockings were credited with being the first team to routinely use the hit-and-run play, with King Kelly, a remarkably innovative player, initiating the action. Kelly came from Paterson, New Jersey, where he grew up with Big Jim McCormick, Silver Flint, The Only Nolan and Johnny Farrell, all of whom became leaders of their teams. Some of the original White Stockings came from the old NA Boston champion team where taskmaster Harry Wright had drilled them on the intricacies of the National Pastime. Maybe they learned the play from him or from each other.

The First World Series Ended on a Home Run

The Ultimate Thrill

1960

BELOW: No one who watched the 1960 World Series will ever forget the drama, as Bill Mazeroski belted the Series-winning homer. The Yankees set new records for runs, hits and home runs, but lost in seven games to the Pirates.

Bill Mazeroski's ninth-inning home run sailed over the head of Yankee left fielder Yogi Berra. The blow won the 1960 World Series for the Pirates, despite the Yankees having set new Series records for hits, runs and home runs. Not to be outdone by the hitters, New York pitcher Whitey Ford had tossed two shutouts en route to his record World Series scoreless streak. In the face of record performances, the Pirates played better defensive ball, Bucco ace Vernon Law won his two starts, and reliever Elroy Face saved the first three victories. At the end of six games, the Series was tied. In the finale, both sides exchanged three-run homers and great plays. Pittsburgh seemingly had the game won by scoring five runs in the eighth inning. However, Bob Friend could not hold the lead as the Yankees tied the score again with two more runs in the top of the ninth. Mazeroski, the leadoff batter in the bottom of the ninth, broke the 9-9 tie with a towering home run shot to left. It was more than a winning hit in the bottom of the ninth, it was the last hurrah of the *ancien regime*. The eight-team leagues, wool uniforms, beanballs, 400 special players (25 players times 16 clubs), and wily general managers taking advantage of country boys never existed again.

Remember Joe Carter circling the bases — jumping with joy, flying through the air with his feet barely on the ground — when he walloped the home run that won the 1993 World Series for Toronto? It was their second straight World Series triumph. While newspapers, tabloids and television commentators reported the happenings off the field, the 1993 Series showed that the game was alive and well.

The seemingly impossible has sometimes become possible in real life diamond action. Don Larsen pitched a perfect game for the Yankees in the 1956 World Series, after being knocked from the box in the previous start. The 1951 Giants won the pennant despite trailing the Dodgers by 13½ games in August and 4-2 in the ninth inning of the final playoff game of the season. With one out and two on, Bobby Thomson lifted a high fly to left that sailed into the stands, giving the Giants a 5-4 victory and baseball another unbelievable finish that made the game half-real and half-fantasy.

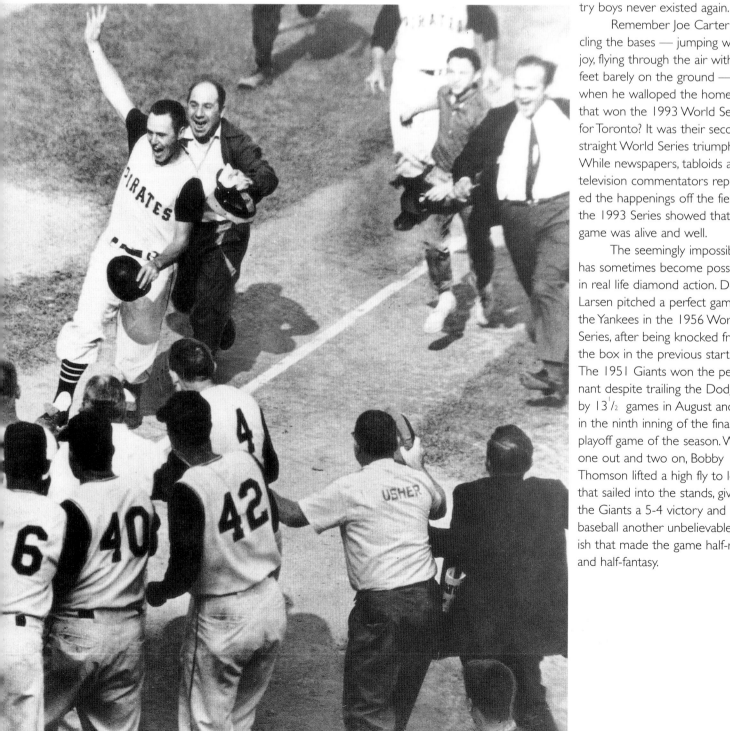

TOP AND BOTTOM LEFT: Bobby Thomson's home run in the ninth inning touched off a wild celebration at home plate and gave the 1951 Giants the pennant.

BOTTOM RIGHT: Joe Carter receives his due after his dinger won the 1993 World Series for the Toronto Blue Jays.

The First World Series Most Valuable Player
The Hero's Honor

1949

RIGHT: Livan Hernandez holds aloft the World Series MVP trophy won in 1997.
BOTTOM LEFT: Reggie Jackson earned his sobriquet "Mr. October" with sterling post-season performances.
BOTTOM RIGHT: Yankee relief ace Joe Page won the first World Series MVP Award for his 1949 performances.

The old *Spalding* and *Reach Guides* used to list "World Series Heroes at a Glance." The listing was similar to a retroactive World Series MVP selection. The current MVP Award came into existence in 1949 when sportswriters picked Yankee relief ace Joe Page as the Series MVP for his three appearances that netted one win and one save with a 2.00 ERA, leading the New Yorkers to beat Brooklyn four games to one. Page's performances showed how unsung heroes could rise to greatness when the occasion presented itself.

One of the most unlikely MVPs was Livan Hernandez in the 1997 Series victory by the Florida Marlins. He was a member of the Cuban National team who left his native Cuba in a leaky boat to defect to the United States, where he wanted to play professional baseball. Starting the 1997 season in the Eastern League, Hernandez did not make the Marlins' starting rotation until August after injuries had felled starters Wilson Alvarez and Pat Rapp. The youthful Hernandez looked like a pudgy kid, but he pitched like a grizzled veteran. Using control and savvy he won both his starts in the League Championship Series, then duplicated the feat in the World Series to win MVP honors in both series.

A word must be mentioned about the greatest World Series performance ever, that of Mr. October in 1977. Reggie Jackson, looking resplendent in pinstripes, swatted three home runs, each on the first ball pitched, in Game Five of the World Series against the Dodgers. His triplet shots augmented his 1977 World Series figures to read five home runs, ten runs, eight RBI, .450 batting average, 1.250 slugging average, and an almost .500 on-base percentage — an MVP performance extraordinaire. His home run and slugging marks have yet to be equalled.

Fans and Sportswriters

The First Sportswriters
No Cheering from the Press Box

1850s

Writers from Henry Chadwick, the first recognizable sportswriter, and O. P. Caylor to Dan Daniels and Dick Young have done their utmost to describe the game of baseball. They painted pictures with words. They did more than depict action, they gave baseball "personality." The old-time sportswriters wrote for an audience that was not in attendance at the game. Many were ex-ballplayers, such as Tim Murnane or Sam Crane. Or the writers might have been small fellows who could not play the game, such as Hugh Fullerton and Ken Smith. Sometimes a real stud came along, such as Ernie Lanigan, and the field opened to broader interpretations. The writers wrote the flowery verse that showed off education as well as described action. On the side, they authored dozens of juvenile fiction and fact books. Some sportswriters became league presidents. These include Ban Johnson, Harry Pulliam, John Heydler and Ford Frick. Frick also became commissioner of baseball.

Nineteenth-century sportswriters assembled a predecessor to the Base Ball Writers Association of America (BBWAA) in 1887 called the Reporters' National Association. Its president was George Munson from *The Sporting News*. Vice president was Henry Chadwick (*New York Clipper*). Ren Mulford (*Cincinnati Times-Star*), Frank Brunell (*Cleveland Plain Dealer*), Frank C. Richter (*Sporting Life*) and Joe Pritchard from St. Louis served on the board of directors. Its success was short lived, but the idea of an association held firm and was presented again when the BBWAA was founded in 1908.

Lifetime member Red Smith gave the following rule for sportswriters. "Use the Mother Tongue with respect and don't gush. The first duty is still to tell you who won, concisely and truthfully. If you can manage that gracefully, so much the better." Sportswriters are the life blood of baseball as an industry. If there were no writers there would be no fans. We would all be playing fantasy bridge.

The First Sportswriter to Cover Spring Training
Baseball Correspondent

1887

Charlie Ferguson burst onto the baseball scene as an extremely talented young man. In addition to winning 99 games in four years, he batted .288 and was paid three bucks a day by A. M. Gillam of the *Philadelphia Record* to cover spring training in 1887. He delivered short bulletins on training camp activities by wire to the Philadelphia newspaper. Ferguson died the next spring, but his deeds off the field live on as spring training coverage made baseball the much anticipated sport that it is. His deeds on the field were portrayed in a restaurant called Charlie Ferguson's in his birthplace of Charlottesville, Virginia. The hip night club featured photos of the old National League star and coeds who never heard of Charlie Ferguson, the pitcher.

By the 1890s the South was overrun each spring by enthusiastic young men practicing fielding, throwing and hitting, and grizzled former players writing for the big city newspapers about the extraordinary chances of the home team in this year's pennant race. Many baseball books were written from gossip acquired during spring training. The venerable Fred Lieb, who may have been the best baseball book writer ever, penned several of the team histories for the Putnam Series during the war and after. His detail of spring training incidents made the players come alive as human beings.

Spring baseball still sells newspapers; just ask *USA Today*. Every team is a potential pennant winner in spring training. Fans want to know and sportswriters, sending missives back from the sunny climes, are the ones in the know.

Copyright 1887.
Goodwin & Co.

Ferguson, P. Philadelph

The First Appearance of *Casey at the Bat*

A Poet and a Thespian

1888

TOP LEFT: William DeWolf Hopper recited *Casey at the Bat* for the New York Giants and Chicago White Stockings in 1888. He did it again the next night when members of the Giants returned.

TOP RIGHT: The attractive Hedda Hopper used husband Hopper to entertain at her lavish parties.

William DeWolf Hopper, a young actor at Wallack's Theatre in New York City, learned that the New York Giants and Chicago White Stockings baseball clubs would be attending a performance of *Prince Methusalem* as guests of the theatre's management. Hopper wanted to do something special for the players. A friend, Archibald Clavering Gunter, remembered a poem that he had clipped from the *San Francisco Examiner*. That clipping was *Casey at the Bat*.

Hopper recited the work during the *entre-act* and was met with a rousing ovation as "mighty Casey ... struck out." Star catcher Buck Ewing returned the next night with more of his friends who wanted to hear "the base ball poem." *Casey* became part of Hopper's repertoire. By his own count, he recited it more than 10,000 times, experimenting with hundreds of slight variations to keep his mind from wandering. Though he was a young man, he became forever associated with *Casey*. It haunted him through six wives; his fifth was Hollywood socialite Hedda Hopper. Their only child, William, played Paul Drake on the *Perry Mason* TV series. Hopper's friend, Gunter, wrote 39 novels, including the best-selling *Mr. Barnes of New York*, but was known mostly as the man who discovered *Casey*.

Casey at the Bat combined the Harvard literati and the Broadway thespian guild to produce the all-time greatest piece of baseball literature. The two groups had more in common than at first glance.

The First Baseball Card
A Piece of the Action

1868

WAGNER, PITTSBURG

Peck and Snyder was one of the foremost suppliers of athletic equipment when baseball was coming into prominence. The sporting goods firm issued the first three baseball cards that were known. The first was the team card of the 1868 Brooklyn Atlantics, the best of the amateur nines during the 1860s. The following year Peck and Snyder produced the team card for the 1869 Cincinnati Red Stockings, the first wholly professional squad and winners of 88 straight games. The 1870 card was a composite of the Philadelphia Athletics. The two previous cards had been team photographs, thus the card was the first composite team photograph as well as a baseball card. Quickly other forms of baseball cards emerged.

The comic cards, showing players with big heads, skinny bodies and funny faces, illustrate that early baseball was not to be taken too seriously. It was a fun game. Then tobacco became involved. The ballplayers were pictured in more manly poses with intensity penned into their faces. In 1887 America's largest maker of little cigars — more popular than cigarettes — Allen & Ginter issued 34 small sets of 50 cards each. Depicted were ballplayers, runners, wrestlers, cyclists, pedestrians, skaters, pugilists and others. The cards were used as inserts to stiffen the packages and to attract new customers. Soon other tobacco companies employed the same idea. In 1890 Allen & Ginter became a subsidiary of the newly formed American Tobacco Trust. By the 1893 depression the Trust had driven more than 250 companies out of business, and cigarette baseball cards were dropped.

Baseball cards, whether cigarette or bubble gum, created interest outside the ballpark. Cards would be the very first piece of baseball literature that young fans read. They also measured the interest in the national game. When baseball made a resurgence in the late 1980s the price of baseball cards skyrocketed. When the players went on strike and the World Series was cancelled, the price of baseball cards plummeted.

Hurley, Sub.; G. Wright, S. S.; Allison, C.; McVey, R. F.; Leonard, L. F.
Sweasy, 2d B.; Waterman, 3d B.; H. Wright, C. F.; Brainard, P.; Gould, 1st B.

RED STOCKING B. B. CLUB OF CINCINNATI.

The First Baseball Movie

Lights, Camera, Action!

1899

Slugging Hal Chase appeared as himself in an early movie that set the standard for baseball fare — a last-game, final-inning home run to capture the pennant.

None other than Thomas Edison made the first baseball movie in 1899. It was an experimental short that dramatized the poem *Casey at the Bat*. Other early baseball movies were sometimes preposterous and sometimes poignant. *His Last Game* (1909) by Carl Laemmie told the story of an Indian baseball team in Arizona whose star pitcher resisted the efforts of cowboy gamblers to buy his services in throwing a game. *Hal Chase's Home Run* (1911) by Hal Chase starred a real ballplayer. This short had Chase winning the pennant with last-game, last-inning home run heroics. The story resembled the later drama of Bobby Thomson winning the 1951 National League pennant with a home run in the last inning of the last playoff game while trailing by a score of 4-2.

Film marketers influenced film makers, and the need for star players was felt at the box office. Charles "Chief" Bender, Jack Coombs and Rube Oldring plied their baseball and acting talents in *The Baseball Bug* (1911). *Home Run Baker's Double* (1914) featured Frank "Home Run" Baker in a script which followed the Hal Chase movie, while Christy Mathewson predated the Bull Durham love story in *Love and Baseball* (1914). Mathewson played the romantic and athletic leads. The only real clunker among early baseball cinema was the regrettable *Somewhere in Georgia* (1916), in which Ty Cobb rode a mule to the big game. A critic claimed it was "absolutely the worst I've ever seen." Babe Ruth fared better with the critics in *Heading Home* (1920), but struck out with the producers when his $50,000 check bounced.

The First Game
Broadcast on Radio

Here's the Wind-up ... and the Pitch!

1921

In 1921 when Harold Arlin introduced baseball to radio audiences, a match made in heaven resulted. Baseball is still the number one radio sport.

The real pioneer of baseball on the radio was KDKA out of Pittsburgh. While the extent of their reach wasn't known, they hired Harold Arlin to broadcast the August 5, 1921, contest between the Pirates and Phillies. The Pirates won the game with three runs in the eighth inning for an 8-5 victory. Arlin, the future grandfather of San Diego Padre right-hander Steve Arlin, had performed baseball's first radio broadcast.

Baseball appeared to be made for radio. The action on the diamond was perfect for creating pictures in the mind. By the beginning of the 1930s most midwestern clubs had regular announcers with whom the listening audience could identify. Ex-player Jack Graney was in Cleveland, Fred Hooey was a fixture on Boston radio, and France Laux on KMOX in St. Louis. Later, ex-Gashouse Gang members Dizzy Dean and Frank Frisch tried their hands at radio, as did Ronald Reagan and Ward Bond.

The First Broadcast
of a World Series Game

Subway Series

1921

TOP LEFT: John McGraw reached the acme of his career with the 1921–1924 NL champion Giants. They played in the first World Series broadcast.

TOP RIGHT: Grantland Rice sat at the microphone for the first World Series broadcast.

What a time and what a place was New York City in the 1920s. The United States with its factories and fresh troops had thwarted German aggression and forced an end to the Great War. New York, as the leading city in the victorious country, saw hordes of fresh new faces, bringing in fresh new ideas. Immigrants and citizens alike saw the 1920s as a time to rejoice and celebrate. The full bloom of the machine age had given workers time and money to take outings to the country or to the ballpark.

In New York, two dynasties were building simultaneously. In the National League John McGraw had retooled the Giants and he would reach the zenith of his career with four straight pennants, 1921-24. Meanwhile in the American League, Colonel Ruppert was acquiring such ballplayers as Babe Ruth, Bob Shawkey, Frank Baker, Herb Pennock and Bob Meusel, who would lead his Yankees to three straight pennants. When both New York clubs won their leagues in 1921, the fans eagerly awaited the World Series.

To the fans' surprise, KDKA out of Pittsburgh announced that they would broadcast Game One of the 1921 Series. Grantland Rice was at the microphone. Even though the first game was the only one broadcast, the experiment was a success. Hooking up baseball with the most modern technology available set a precedent that would continue to benefit baseball in the future.

The national game can hold sway over the most intelligent and innovative of people. The availability of baseball on the Internet is a direct link to baseball's access on radio, the most modern form of communications of the period.

The First Televised Game
A New Genre

1939

Red Barber interviews Leo
Durocher at Ebbets Field
before the initial major
league baseball telecast on
August 23, 1939.

Bill Stern, Mr. Sports in New York City before the war,
broadcast the first televised baseball game on May 17,
1939. The contest between Princeton and Columbia —
won by Princeton 2-1 in 10 innings — was viewed from
a single camera on a stationary post. The lens pointed toward
home plate and announcer Bill Stern was expected to fill in the
rest of the play-by-play action. He later recounted that his
prayers asked for every out to be a strikeout. The *New York
Times* reviewed the broadcast with, "it is difficult to see how this
sort of thing can catch the public fancy."

Thinking that the lack of interest related to college baseball,
Red Barber broadcast a doubleheader from Ebbets Field on
August 26, 1939, over W2XBS. The first contest went to the
Dodgers 6-2, while the Reds captured the second 5-1. Soon
baseball fans would be watching the *Game of the Week*, starring
Dizzy Dean and various sidekicks.

The First Company to Sponsor Pro Baseball

Mutual Interest

1869

Ted Turner, a pioneer of television superstations, celebrates his Atlanta Braves' World Series triumph in 1995.

Baseball must attract big bucks to stay on top of the sports world. Disney's purchase of the Anaheim Angels shows the rest of big business that one of the biggest thinks baseball is a good buy. In 1990s the words "corporate sponsorship" echoed the great hope for baseball as the ownership of clubs changed from families such as the Wrigleys and O'Malleys. Dan Topping and Del Webb started the move to corporate ownership by selling the New York Yankees to the CBS network during the 1960s. Since that time, P. K. Wrigley sold the Chicago Cubs to the *Chicago Tribune*, who also owned WGN television network. Ted Turner allowed his Atlanta Braves to grow with his CNN and TBS television networks. Wealthy individuals continued to own ball clubs, but the 1970s idea of linking such principle companies as Marion Laboratories with the Kansas City Royals or American Ship Building with the Yankees fell into disuse during the 1990s when a new form of corporate sponsorship came into being. Blockbuster Video's Wayne Huizinga won a World Series with the expansion Florida Marlins, and the corporate board of Walt Disney Enterprises purchased the Anaheim Angels. The CEO of Walmart acquired control of the Kansas City Royals, and Walmart became a corporate sponsor of Major League Baseball. If such sponsorship was beneficial to the game wouldn't it have appeared at the beginning?

The original Cincinnati Red Stockings from 1869 featured correspondent Harry M. Millar from the *Cincinnati Commercial*, who accompanied the team on the road and wrote stories which were telegraphed back to Cincinnati via Western Union telegraph cables. On the western trip officials from Western Union accompanied the team. It may be said that Western Union was the first corporate sponsor of pro baseball. By 1879 every large to medium sized city had Western Union wire offices with special reporting times for baseball scores.

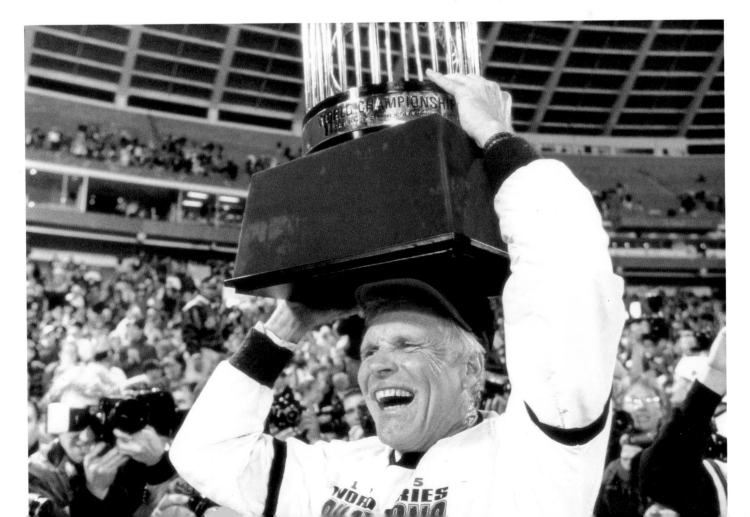

The First Baseball Reference Books
The Scoop

1868

BELOW: In 1888 John M. Ward wrote an early baseball "how-to" book.
BELOW RIGHT: President of the National Association of Professional Baseball Leagues, George Trautman wrote a marketing guide.

Henry Chadwick started editing Erastus Beadle's (the inventor of the dime novel) *Dime Baseball Player* in 1860. The annual guide provided detailed information on the history of the game, and on the rules and regulations. The booklet gave instructions on how to form a baseball club, then how to choose the playing field, and how to choose the players for each position. A section on scorekeeping followed the advice on how to choose a scorer. The readers also received annual reports on the important clubs, their records and their statistics. Chadwick put his research and beliefs into *The Game of Baseball: How to Learn It, How to Play It, and How to Teach It*. Published in 1868, it told the story of baseball and gave readers brief sketches of players and instructional techniques on how to play the game that would eventually become the National Pastime. His *Technical Terms of Baseball* (1887) was the first glossary of baseball idioms. The inside poop on how to play effectively made John Montgomery Ward's *Base-Ball: How to Become a Player, with the Origin, History, and Explanation of the Game* (1888) a book for the ages. What was true in 1888 was still true in 1988. Fred Pfeffer's *Scientific Base Ball* (1889) was a ballplayer's thoughts on the game.

In 1890 the Midwestern weekly, *The Sporting News*, became a publishing giant overnight when it broke the stunning story of the formation of the Players' League. The four-year-old baseball newspaper used the media opportunity to boost its national circulation to compete effectively against *Sporting Life*, an East Coast sporting paper first published in 1883.

Baseball research was also a staple of the book publishing industry. Ernie Lanigan edited the first encyclopedia of baseball information. He called it *Cyclopedia* (1921). Its format was nearly the same as that of *The Official Encyclopedia of Baseball* (1948) by Sherley C. Thompson and Hy Turkin. Then came the blockbuster that exploded baseball knowledge.

When the commissioner's office was contacted about a baseball statistical project, National League attorney Bowie Kuhn saw the possibilities of a complete baseball reference. Then Kuhn became commissioner and the Macmillan Publishing Company had a baseball official on their side. Bowie Kuhn enthusiastically endorsed *The Baseball Encyclopedia* (1969). The book spawned dozens of publications, in book and periodical form, with supporting data from the complete career records of every person who played major league baseball, including another popular and reliable reference, *Total Baseball*.

The First Hall of Fame Induction

The Flying Dutchman, Big Six, the Big Train, the Georgia Peach, and the Babe

BELOW: In 1939, 10 of the 11 living members of the Hall of Fame gathered for a photo. Ty Cobb arrived too late.

BOTTOM: At his induction in 1989, Carl Yastrzemski is honored by Commissioner A. Bartlett Giamatti.

Local citizens in Cooperstown, New York, wanted to stage the celebration of baseball's 100th anniversary on their ball diamond, Doubleday Field. They felt the occasion could validate the findings of the Mills Commission, first published in 1908, which stated that baseball had its origin in a pasture of Green's Select School near Cooperstown. A deceased Union Army general named Abner Doubleday was given credit for laying out the diamond and teaching a group of boys the rules of the game. Even though recent research has shown that events could never have happened as stated, the town fathers saw the significance of the Mills report of Cooperstown. They started during the early 1920s to raise money for the 1939 celebration. When the Depression hit and fundraising bogged down, local philanthropist Stephen Clark contacted Commissioner K. M. Landis and National League President Ford Frick, both of whom endorsed the idea. They planned to turn it into a celebration of baseball itself.

Frick, a BBWAA card holder, convinced the Baseball Writers Association of America to cast votes to pick the all-time greatest players to be honored in a Hall of Fame. In 1936 they chose Ty Cobb, Babe Ruth, Christy Mathewson, Honus Wagner and Walter Johnson as the first honorees. Commissioner Landis and NL President Frick actively campaigned for a Hall to be built in Cooperstown, New York, where local activity had been limited to preparing a baseball field for baseball's 100th anniversary celebration. Soon baseball memorabilia came pouring in from excited players and fans. So many items arrived that plans were drawn for building a museum of baseball history.

Other inductees of the thirties — Nap Lajoie, Tris Speaker, Cy Young, George Wright, Ban Johnson, Connie Mack, Morgan Bulkeley, John McGraw, Grover C. Alexander, Alexander Cartwright, Henry Chadwick, George Sisler, Eddie Collins, Willie Keeler, Cap Anson, Charles Comiskey, Candy Cummings, Buck Ewing, Old Hoss Radbourn and Al Spalding — joined the original honorees as Hall of Famers. Lou Gehrig was selected in a special election, waiving the rules. Newcomers of 1939 Eddie Collins and George Sisler joined the nine living immortals in attending the induction service at the museum dedication in Cooperstown, New York. The National Baseball Library was opened on the second floor.

The Baseball Hall of Fame celebrated its 50th anniversary in 1989 with year-long promotions, national advertising and a book of the museum's treasures. The summer's activities included town ball exhibitions and the annual induction. That year supporters of inductees Carl Yastrzemski, Johnny Bench, Red Schoendienst, and Al Barlick flooded into the picturesque village. Induction weekend, which featured a game in Doubleday Field between two major league teams, highlighted the year, which was marked by the greatest attendance in the history of the Hall of Fame — more than 400,000 in a village of 2,500 — and significant changes in the town itself. An opera house was built on the banks of Cooperstown's Otsego Lake. Many new businesses, all related to baseball, sprung up on the town's Main Street, and a trolley system was inaugurated to handle the transportation of visitors. Baseball historian John Thorn said of Cooperstown, "If baseball wasn't invented here, it should have been."

The First Player Stalked by a Fan
Fan-a-tic

1949

Ruth Steinhagen (left) is found to be insane and sentenced to life in a mental institution while her mother and father, and wheelchair-bound Eddie Waitkus, listen to the state's attorney John S. Boyle (right).

Shock was the reaction of the Philadelphia Phillies players and fans when they heard about Ruth Steinhagen shooting their first baseman Eddie Waitkus. The 1949 shooting inspired a fictionalization in Bernard Malamud's 1952 novel *The Natural,* and portrayed on the silver screen by Robert Redford in 1984. "Baby, why did you do it?" was all Waitkus could say when, responding to a note, he went to the hotel room of 19-year-old Steinhagen after a game and she pulled a rifle and shot him.

Steinhagen had never spoken to him, never gotten his autograph, but she had spent a lot of time at Wrigley Field following her first spotting of Waitkus in 1947 when he played for the Cubs. She quickly became obsessed, learning to speak Lithuanian to better understand his ancestry. She collected Waitkus photographs and Waitkus news articles. She sat in her room and listened to records made in 1936, because Eddie wore number 36 on the back of his uniform. When he was traded to Philadelphia, Steinhagen could not handle the change. She shot him because, "If I couldn't have him, neither could anybody else." Fortunately, Waitkus recovered and even made a comeback, playing major league ball for another six years.

Ballplayers are subject to the same vulnerabilities as any other public figures. More than four decades after the Waitkus shooting, an armed female fan was arrested at the Toronto SkyDome — without incident — for stalking the Blue Jays' star player Roberto Alomar.

Travel

The First Road Trip
The 1860 Excelsiors

1860

The Excelsior Base Ball
Club of Brooklyn with
Jim Creighton, third from
left, excited ball fans
during their 1860 road trip
the same way that the
New York Yankees thrilled
crowds in 1998.

Jim Creighton, from the first electric moment that he took
the pitcher's box in baseball's early days, thrilled crowds. Men,
women and boys traveled many miles by horseback and ox
cart, or the old-fashioned nineteenth-century bipedal mode,
to see him and the Brooklyn Excelsiors play. No one had
ever seen a pitched ball delivered so swiftly and so accurately.
What a gate attraction he was!!

The messieurs who ran the Excelsior Base Ball Club took
the unprecedented step of sending their top nine players on a
road trip to upstate New York. Albany, the first stop on July 2,
1860, was the first opponent to go down, 24-6. Troy met with
defeat 13-7, an exceptionally well-played game for the era.
Buffalo suffered a 50-19 defeat. Two Rochester clubs went down
21-1 and 27-9. The Excelsiors returned home by way of
Newburg, New York, where the locals succumbed 59-14. The
success of this trip led to another, but toward the South.

Hostilities between the North and South had not yet broken out and the country was baseball crazy. The second trip
took place during late July and transported the team to
Baltimore and Philadelphia. The fans turned out to see the
famous Jim Creighton, but also to compare their style of baseball to the kind played in Brooklyn.

The First Teams to Travel Abroad

Cricket, Anyone?

1874

When the National Association was the major league, league rules required that each team schedule so many series against each opponent. Since no document declared when those games had to be played, the Boston Red Stockings and Philadelphia Athletics packed their gear and went to England July 16 through August 16 of 1874. The trip, arranged by Boston pitcher Albert Spalding, was expected to engage the two American clubs in a series of baseball exhibition contests with English nines, but the English wanted to play cricket instead of baseball. The American nines, led by Athletics pitcher Dick McBride and Red Stockings mentor Harry Wright — both able and tested bowlers — annihilated the English clubs on the cricket field. McBride and his fireballs even torched the famed Marylebone Cricket Club. The key to the Yanks' success laid in waiting for a pitch (bowl) they could drive past the fielders. The English, who faithfully swung at every bowl, whether it hit the wicket or not, charged the Americans with "dirty cricket." Al Spalding turned his sights toward another, grander tour, one that might include financial gain.

Spalding was ahead of his time, trying to open Europe and overseas possessions to the sports marketplace. One hundred years later the moguls of baseball have only begun to fully implement the ideas of long-past leaders.

The First Teams to Go Around the World
Baseball Under the Pyramids

1888-1889

TOP: Al Spalding, with a safari hat, posed with local government officials in the Egyptian desert during the 1888 tour.
BELOW: An 1888 shot of the Great Sphinx includes members of the Spalding tour.

In *Innocents Abroad*, Mark Twain described his chance meeting in Eygpt with the Chicago and All-America traveling baseball teams. He was awakened by an Egyptian boy who screamed, "The Americans are climbing on the antiquities." Twain rushed out to the area and saw baseball players laying out a diamond at the foot of the Great Pyramid of Cheops. He was relieved to see Egyptian government officials supervising the temporary construction. The two nines usually played on cricket grounds during their tour.

Remembering the fun he had had in 1874 when his Boston club went to England, Al Spalding put together a baseball exhibition trip in 1888 to Australia via the Sandwich Islands, this time featuring an All-American and a Chicago squad. There they met Alexander Cartwright, who had laid out the Knickerbockers' diamond in the 1840s. Cartwright did not get to see the teams play because of the Sunday labor laws. From there they sailed to Australia, Ceylon, Cairo, Rome, Florence, Paris and England, where the travelers finished their series. The final standings showed that Chicago had won 13 games and the All-American squad 17. More than 60,000 people had witnessed the exhibitions in England alone. The All-Americans, under union leader John M. Ward, won eight of the last twelve games after hearing that the Brush Classification Plan (a nineteenth-century salary cap) had been approved by the stateside owners.

The most amusing story from the trip was told by Cap Anson in *A Ball Player's Career*. He wrote that the two teams had booked passage on a German freighter for the portion of the trip, Australia to Ceylon. The Teutonic crew and captain spoke no English, but Fred Pfeffer of the All-Americans conversed in fluent German. Pfeffer and his friends spent the entire voyage dining with the vessel's commander while Spalding and the rest ate with the deckhands down below.

The trip proved that baseball could be played anywhere and that Americans were unflappable in their crazed enthusiasm for the game. Tour leader Al Spalding boasted that every country touched by the baseball tourists fought on the Allied side in World War I. Many of those countries also became part of the worldwide Spalding marketplace.

The First Team to Go South for Spring Training

Way Down Yonder

1870

Bert Niehoff, John McGraw and Roy Schalk talk at spring training in Texas with the 1929 Giants. The Giants and McGraw drew big crowds in Dallas, Ft. Worth, Oklahoma City, Tulsa and Kansas City as the team headed north.

Teams went south during spring training for one basic reason, which was to play baseball in warm weather. Side benefits were paying crowds, hot springs and publicity. Spring training cost money. Players were not even paid during the pre-season games until a lawyer named Robert Murphy attempted to organize a union in 1946. In order to buy off the players, baseball moguls gave their minions a stipend for spring training. For many years, this payment was known as "Murphy money." After owners paid their players for spring training, they sought to recoup their expenses through a schedule of spring games with other organizations. In the money grab the real reason for spring training was lost.

The Cincinnati Reds and Chicago White Stockings went south in 1870 to prepare for the upcoming season and to play each other in front of southern crowds who could not otherwise see the nation's top professionals in action. Later, Chicago returned south and went to Hot Springs, Arkansas. The athletes felt that the mineral waters purified their bodies after a winter on the rich food and wine circuit. The White Stockings sent teammates south in 1885 and 1886. Winning pennants both years, they prompted their opponents to go south themselves.

The First Baseball Teams from Japan to Tour the USA
Asian Connection

1905

The Waseda University baseball team was the first from Japan to tour the United States.

Many years ago students from the leading universities of the Japanese empire adopted baseball as their most popular form of outdoor pastime. Some historians have placed the wreath of initiation on Horace Wilson, a professor in Tokyo during the 1870s. By the turn of the century Keio University and Waseda Imperial University had both organized strong teams and had played frequent matches, often attracting thousands of enthusiastic patrons. Twice teams from Waseda University visited the United States.

Waseda University and a team composed of American Indians for the Sherman Government Institute of California played at Fiesta Park in Los Angeles on May 20, 1905. The Japanese won 12-7. It was the third game of their tour, but the first written up by *Sporting Life*. Waseda split two previous engagements with Los Angeles High School, 5-3 and 5-6. Kono, the ironman pitcher for Waseda, hurled all three contests. The Waseda Imperial team was coached by American Frank Merrifield, who was an instructor at the University. After completing the schedule in California the Imperialists went to Chicago.

In a reciprocal move, in the fall of 1909 students from the University of Wisconsin played a nine-game schedule in Japan that had been pre-arranged by their hosts, the Athletic Association of Keio University. The American boys proved to be good guests by losing three of four to the Japanese champion Keio nine before they easily defeated Tokyo University in two games. Two years later, another team from Waseda University visited the U.S.

The First Pro Team to Tour Japan
East met West

1913

BELOW: In Tokyo 65,000 fans watched Babe Ruth take batting practice at Meiji Shrine Stadium prior to the game on November 4, 1934.
BOTTOM: Babe Ruth was a hero in Japan as well as in the United States.

Although many amateur teams visited the land of the Rising Sun, the first professionals did not show up until November 1913, when players from the New York Giants and Chicago White Sox included Japan in their globe-circling exhibition jaunt. The combined clubs played two games, a third rained out, against the better Japanese college clubs and won 16-3 and 12-3. Other tours' junkets included big league players.

In 1922 a big league all-star team including Casey Stengel was organized by major league baseball under the auspices of Herbert Hunter. Judge Landis picked and scrutinized the touring professionals. He forced players to undergo moral scrutiny in order to represent U.S. baseball overseas. Nine years later, another group, many of whom took their wives, embarked for Japan. The big leaguers were Lou Gehrig, Lefty Grove, Frank Frisch, Mickey Cochrane, Lefty O'Doul, and many others. They toured the island and set the stage for the biggest event in Japanese-United States baseball history.

Babe Ruth and the great tour arrived at the Imperial island in 1934. Matsutaro Shoriki, owner of the Yomiuri newspapers, sponsored the tour. The trip would send Japan toward a baseball future and Shoriki would drive it. Ruth and the other great stars played 18 games and easily won 17 of them. The other was set against a team featuring high school pitcher Eiji Sawamura, who almost shut them out, striking out Charlie Gehringer, Ruth, Gehrig, and Jimmie Foxx in succession before losing 1-0. Sawamura became a household name in Japan. His hero status was solidified when he plunged to a fiery death as a kamikaze pilot during World War II. To honor the baseball war hero, Japanese officials named the award for the outstanding pitcher of the year, the Eiji Sawamura Award.

Subject Guide

THE GAME

Picture Credits